INFORMIX Press

INFORMIX

Performance

Tuning

INFORMIX Press

INFORMIX

Performance

Tuning

Second Edition

Elizabeth Suto

Prentice Hall PTR
Upper Saddle River, NJ 07458
http://www.prenhall.com

To join a Prentice Hall PTR
mailing list, point to:
http://www.prenhall.com/register

Library of Congress Cataloging-in-Publication Data

```
Suto Elizabeth,
      Informix performance tuning / Elizabeth Suto. — 2nd ed.
         p.  cm.
      First ed. published under title: Informix-online performance tuning,
   c1995.
      Includes index.
   ISBN 0-13-239237-2
      1. Database management. 2. Informix-OnLine. 3. Client/server
   computing. I. Suto, Elizabeth. Informix-online performance tuning. II.
   Title
   QA76.9.D3S9415  1997
   005'.75'8—dc20                                          96-46682
                                                              CIP
```


Editorial/production supervision: *BooksCraft, Inc., Indianapolis, IN*
Cover design director: *Jerry Votta*
Cover design: *Karen Marsilio*
Acquisitions editor: *Mark L. Taub*
Marketing manager: *Dan Rush*

Manager, Informix Press: *Todd Katz*
Founder, Informix Press: *Suzanne Fuery*

© 1997 by Prentice Hall PTR
Prentice-Hall, Inc.
A Simon & Schuster Company
Upper Saddle River, NJ 07458

Informix Press
Informix® Software, Inc.
4100 Bohannon Drive
Menlo Park, CA 94025

The publisher offers discounts on this book when ordered in bulk quantities.
For more information, contact:

Corporate Sales Department, Prentice Hall PTR, One Lake Street, Upper Saddle River, NJ 07458
Phone: 800-382-3419   Fax: 201-236-7141   E-mail: corpsales@prenhall.com

The following are worldwide trademarks of Informix Software, Inc., or its subsidiaries, registered in the United States as indicated by "®" and in numerous other countries worldwide: INFORMIX-OnLine®, INFORMIX-SE®, and INFORMIX-SQL.®

Printed in the United States of America

10 9 8 7 6 5 4 3 2 1

ISBN: 0-13-239237-2

Prentice-Hall International (UK) Limited, *London*
Prentice-Hall of Australia Pty. Limited, *Sydney*
Prentice-Hall Canada Inc., *Toronto*
Prentice-Hall Hispanoamericana, S.A., *Mexico*
Prentice-Hall of India Private Limited, *New Delhi*
Prentice-Hall of Japan, Inc., *Tokyo*
Simon & Schuster Asia Pte. Ltd., *Singapore*
Editora Prentice-Hall do Brasil, Ltda., *Rio de Janeiro*

Table of Contents

▟▙ INFORMIX®
Press

INFORMIX
Performance
Tuning

Chapter 1

Introduction to INFORMIX-OnLine and INFORMIX-OnLine Dynamic Server

The purpose of this chapter is to give new administrators the minimum amount of information necessary to understand the rest of the chapters in this book. The OnLine database server is somewhat complex and carries its own terminology. However, with a basic knowledge, you can perform basic monitoring and tuning tasks.

This book discusses two versions of the database server: INFORMIX-OnLine and INFORMIX-OnLine Dynamic Server. INFORMIX-OnLine is the earlier version of the server, and we will discuss features up to and including the 5.02 release. The INFORMIX-OnLine Dynamic Server is the later release, which contains substantial internal redesign to improve scalability and parallel query performance. We will discuss performance features in versions up to and including the 7.12 release.

The distinctions between INFORMIX-OnLine and INFORMIX-OnLine Dynamic Server are pointed out in all chapters of the book. When a feature or behavior is similar in both versions, the server is referred to as "OnLine" or "the database server" for simplicity.

Before delving into performance issues, it is important to know the basic architecture of the database server. The topics covered in this chapter are

- Overview of the INFORMIX-OnLine and INFORMIX-OnLine Dynamic Server architectures
- Processing an SQL statement
- Checkpoints and logging
- Client/server communication
- Multiple OnLine systems

1.1   OVERVIEW OF THE ONLINE ARCHITECTURE

OnLine is a database server, which means that it acts as a liaison between a user and a database. OnLine is responsible for reading and writing data to and from the database, controlling and optimizing access to the database, and protecting and preserving the integrity of the data.

Disk, memory, and processes together make up what is known as the *OnLine system* or *database server*, although it is actually the processes within the system that are doing the work.

INFORMIX-OnLine Process Architecture

INFORMIX-OnLine is based on a two-process model. The first process, the client application, is responsible for all interaction with the user via a user interface. When an application encounters an SQL statement, it passes that statement to the second process, the database server, via the UNIX Inter-Process Communication (IPC) pipes mechanism. The database server (the process name is **sqlturbo**) is responsible for parsing, optimizing, and executing the SQL statement, retrieving any requested data and passing the data back to the application (see Fig. 1.1).

Figure 1.1-The INFORMIX-OnLine process architecture

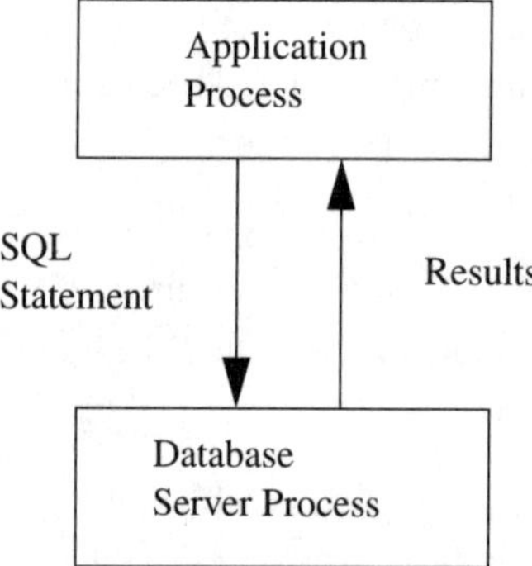

For every user, there are two processes. The application process can run either on the same machine as the database server process or on another "client" machine. Although this architecture works well with fewer users, with hundreds of users, the large number of processes consumes the operating system, which has to handle context switching among all the processes.

INFORMIX-OnLine Dynamic Server Process Architecture

INFORMIX-OnLine Dynamic Server is fundamentally different from previous versions because it uses a multithreaded architecture (see Fig. 1.2). In this version, fewer processes can handle the work load of hundreds, even thousands of users. These database server processes are called *virtual processors*, or *vps*. A vp belongs to a *vp class*, which has a responsibility for a set of tasks. For example, the AIO (asynchronous I/O) vps are responsible for all nonlogging I/O. The CPU vps handle most of the CPU-intensive work.

Figure 1.2-The INFORMIX-OnLine Database Server process architecture

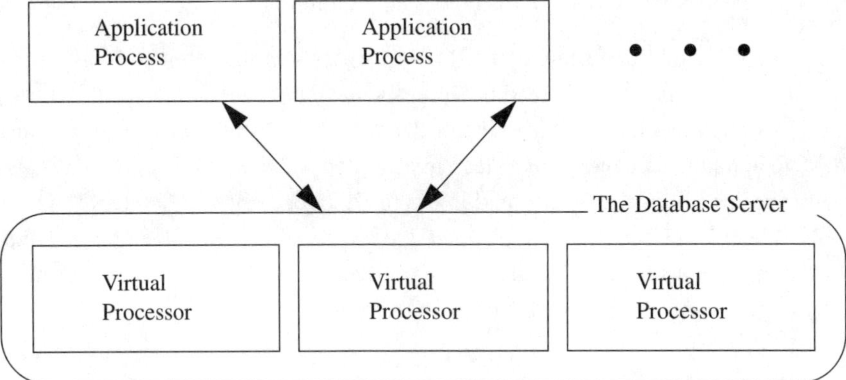

The virtual processors are normal UNIX processes—these processes make up the database server, or OnLine system.

A *thread* is an entity in a virtual processor that has its own context, meaning its own pointer to a place in the code (program counter) and its own data variables. At any one time, only one thread within the process is running, while the others must wait. A multithreaded process cuts down on the operating system overhead, as UNIX sees and administers only one process. You can think of a thread as "taking over" the process when it runs. When the thread completes its work, the thread lets another thread "take over" the process. In this way, one process is running on behalf of more than one user. All the multithreading activities are internal to the INFORMIX database server.

Each application process connecting to the database server is known as a *session*. The session has one or more threads associated with it. The threads are responsible for executing the SQL statements requested by the application.

A session thread runs on vps in the CPU vp class. It can migrate across any CPU vp, which keeps a vp from getting tied up with a single thread. All CPU vps take threads that are ready to run from the same ready queue.

When a session thread must wait for any reason (such as for a lock or disk I/O), it performs a *context switch*, which means it yields control of the process to another thread waiting to run in the ready queue. It will put itself on the wait or sleep queue while waiting for the resource. Another vp, called the AIO vp will normally perform the I/O on behalf of the session and wake up the waiting session thread when the I/O has completed.

Note that a thread context switch is similar to a UNIX process context switch, except that less data must be swapped for a thread context switch. Also, the thread context switch is completely transparent to the operating system.

Figure 1.3 shows an example of a thread context switch. Thread 6 is currently running on the virtual processor. Thread 6 requires some data that is on disk, so it must yield the CPU virtual processor while it waits for the disk I/O. Thread 6 sends a read request to the AIO vp and puts its context on a sleep queue (step 1). Next, thread 6 replaces its context with the context of the next thread in the ready queue, thread 33 (step 2). Once this happens, thread 33 effectively controls the CPU virtual processor. When the AIO vp performs the disk read for thread 6, thread 6 is moved from the sleep queue to the ready queue, to wait for an available CPU vp to run (step 3).

Figure 1.3-Thread context switch

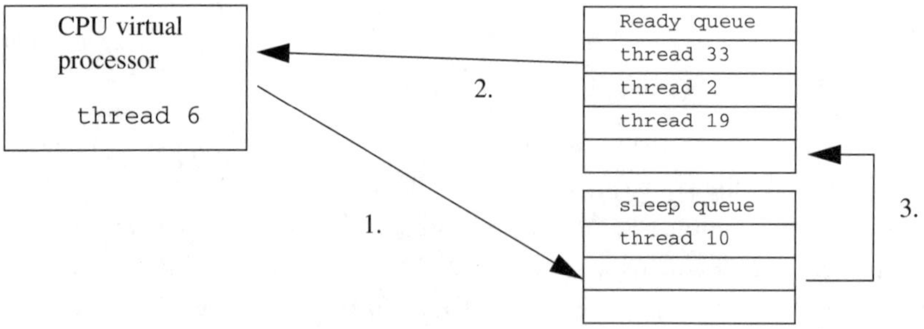

In addition to the CPU vp and the AIO vp, there are several other vp classes:

- **LIO vps.** The LIO vps write transaction log records to the logical log on disk. One LIO vp is automatically started. Two will be started if the disk that has the logical log is mirrored.

- **PIO vps.** The PIO vps write log records to the physical log on disk. One PIO vp is automatically started. Two will be started if the disk that has the physical log is mirrored.

- **ADM vp.** One ADM vp is started as a timer and is responsible for waking up threads that are sleeping for a certain period of time.

- **Network vps (SHM, SOC, TLI).** These vps are usually responsible for polling for requests from client applications. The number and type of network vps are configurable by the administrator.

1.2 DISK TERMINOLOGY

OnLine handles its own disk management. You allocate a set of files or raw device space, and OnLine allocates databases and tables in that space, along with control information and log space. Figure 1.4 gives an example of the components of OnLine disk storage.

You add space to OnLine in large contiguous blocks called *chunks*. Chunks can range from 1 Mbyte to 2 gigabytes in size. A chunk can be a part of a disk or the entire disk. Chunks are allocated in a logical grouping called a *dbspace*. A dbspace represents one or more chunks that are used for a similar purpose. For example, you can place a table in a dbspace, and the rows will be placed in any chunk that is a part of that dbspace.

Chunks are subdivided into *pages*. A page is a fixed contiguous unit of space, usually either 2 or 4 kbytes in size, depending upon the hardware and operating system you

Figure 1.4-Pages, chunks, dbspaces, and extents

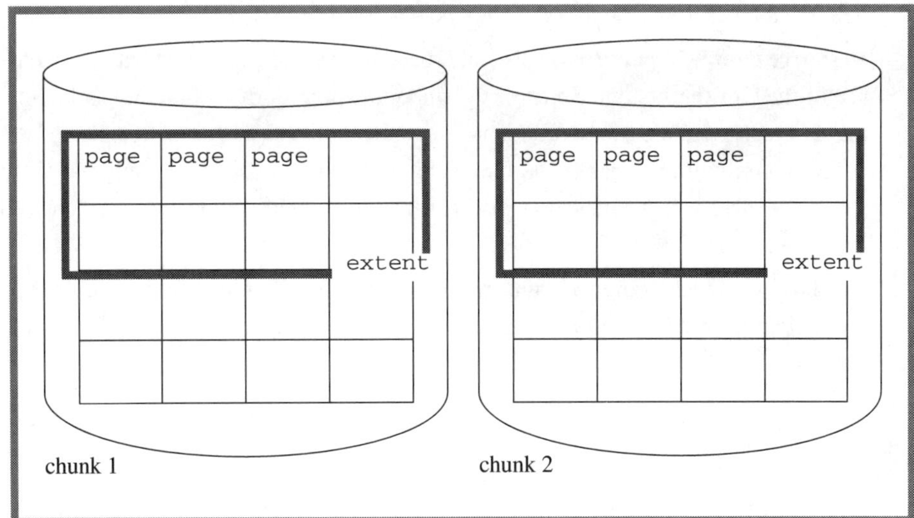

are using. Pages are created to hold certain kinds of information, such as data or indexes. An index does not coexist with the data on the same page.

When a table is created, it is assigned a set of pages to use. Each "set" is physically contiguous within a chunk and is called an *extent*. When these pages fill with data, another extent is allocated on the same or different chunk within the dbspace. Extents are used to group pages from the same table together on a chunk that might contain data and index pages from more than one table.

The extent sizes for each table can be specified with the CREATE TABLE and ALTER TABLE statements. The collection of extents for a table is sometimes referred to as a *tblspace*. Each tblspace has an internal identification number associated with it, called a *tblspace number*.

1.3 SHARED MEMORY

Shared memory is used to hold data structures that the OnLine system uses frequently. Some of the shared memory structures common to both INFORMIX-OnLine and INFOR-MIX-OnLine Dynamic Server are:

- **The buffer cache.** This is usually a substantial area in shared memory where pages on disk are temporarily held. By using pages in memory rather than on disk, you can decrease the number of disk reads and writes that occur. Since the buffer pool is shared by all users, one user can take advantage of a page brought into the buffer pool by another user without performing a disk read.

- **Resource control structures.** This is a broad category of structures that control the use of the OnLine system. Some of the important structures include the lock table, the user table, and the transaction table. You specify the size of these structures by a series of configuration parameters. Starting with version 7.10.UD1, some of these structures (dbspaces, chunks, transactions) are automatically allocated and increased as needed.

- **Log buffers.** The logging mechanism uses some shared memory pages to hold temporary log information before it is sent to disk. You can specify the size of these log buffers through several configuration parameters.

How these shared memory structures can affect performance will be discussed in chapter 5.

INFORMIX-OnLine allocates all of the needed shared memory during the initialization of the OnLine instance. Figure 1.5 shows many of the components of INFORMIX-OnLine shared memory.

Figure 1.5-Shared memory in INFORMIX-OnLine

Lock table	User table	Chunk table	Logical log buffer
Latch table	Transaction table	Dbspace table	Physical log buffer
Buffer cache			

Shared Memory in INFORMIX-OnLine Dynamic Server

In the INFORMIX-OnLine Dynamic Server, the amount of shared memory needed by the OnLine system increases dramatically from INFORMIX-OnLine. This is because the memory normally used by the individual **sqlturbo** processes in INFORMIX-OnLine is implemented in shared memory in the INFORMIX-OnLine Dynamic Server. Shared memory is divided into three separate sets of segments:

- **The resident segments.** These segments hold the same information that was found in INFORMIX-OnLine (see Fig. 1.5), mainly the buffer cache and various shared memory structures.

- **The virtual segments.** These segments hold all the information needed in order to run the threads, such as the thread context. Also, any other memory needed to cache stored procedures or perform a sort is also allocated here. Virtual segments are added as needed while the OnLine system is running.

- **The message segments.** These segments hold messages used in communicating with the application by shared memory Inter-Process Communication (IPC).

1.4   PROCESSING AN SQL STATEMENT

The client application process passes the SQL statement (e.g., INSERT, UPDATE, DELETE, or SELECT) to the database server, which is responsible for parsing, optimizing, and executing the statement and returning the resulting data.

Usually, during the course of executing the statement, data must be read from the database. The database server determines the pages that need to be read to satisfy the SQL statement. If the needed page is in the shared memory buffer cache, it will be read from memory (see Fig. 1.6). If not, the page is read from disk and put in the shared memory buffer cache. Since the buffer cache is shared, other users can access the same page in memory without having to perform a disk read. The more often data are read from memory and not disk, the higher the *read cache rate*. Systems with a high read cache rate are obviously more efficient.

When the SQL statement requires a write to the database (INSERT, UPDATE, or DELETE), the database server will write to the page in the buffer cache. When a page is written in memory, it is marked as *dirty*, meaning it must eventually be copied to disk. The write to disk is put off as long as possible, in hopes that multiple users write to the same page in memory or that a single user writes to the same page in memory multiple times. The more often the same page is written in memory, the higher the *write cache rate*. Systems with a high write cache rate are more efficient.

Figure 1.6-Processing an SQL statement

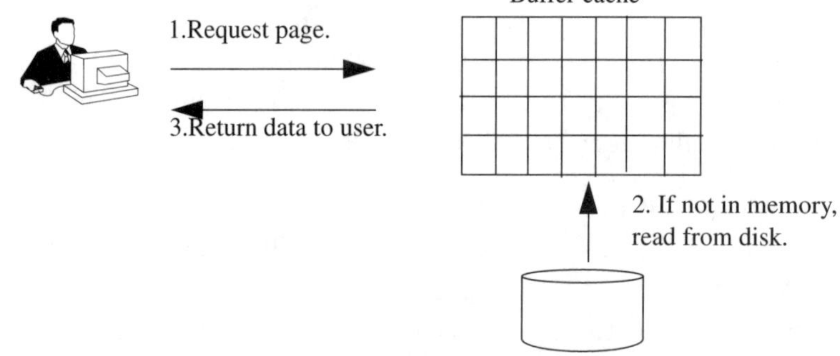

1.5   CHECKPOINTS AND LOGICAL AND PHYSICAL LOGGING

The buffer cache is an important component of the OnLine system because it decreases the amount of disk reads and writes that are necessary in SQL operations. However, by writing to memory rather than disk, we are in danger of losing data that has not yet been committed to disk. OnLine uses three mechanisms to prevent the loss of data: checkpoints, logical logs, and physical logs.

Before writing to a page in memory, the OnLine system does two things:

- It takes a before-image of that page (a copy of the page before it was changed) and writes it to the physical log buffer, which is another area in shared memory. When the physical log buffer is full, it is flushed to an area on disk called the physical log.

- It writes a record of the change in the logical log buffer in shared memory. When this buffer is full, it is flushed to an area on disk called the logical log. The logical log buffer could actually be flushed to disk more often if unbuffered logging is used. Unbuffered logging will be discussed in chapter 3.

Figure 1.7 shows these steps.

Figure 1.7-Logical and physical logging

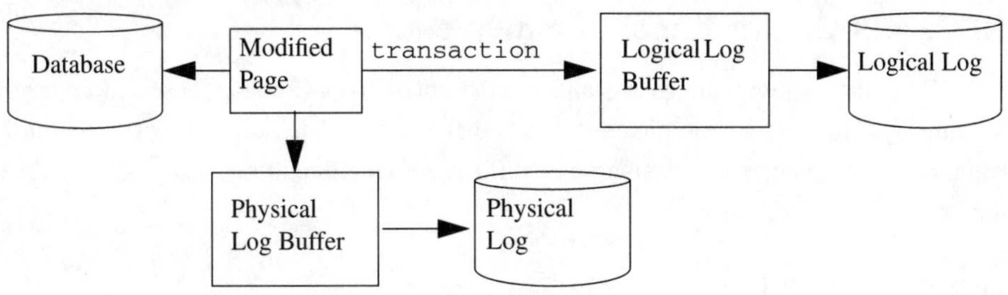

Every few minutes (the actual amount of time is configurable), the OnLine system forces a checkpoint to occur. A *checkpoint* is the synchronization of data that are on disk with data that are in memory. The OnLine system synchronizes data by doing the following:

1. Flush any pages in the physical log buffer to disk.
2. Write to disk all pages that have been modified in memory (dirty pages).
3. Make an entry in the logical log marking the time the checkpoint occurred.
4. Clear the physical log file. The physical log stores pages that have been changed between checkpoints. These pages are no longer necessary once the checkpoint completes.
5. Flush the logical log buffer to disk.

The logical log, the physical log, and the checkpoint are all used for recovery. Suppose the OnLine system goes down during a heavy period of activity. Since data in memory has most certainly been altered, OnLine must recover to a point where all incomplete transactions are rolled back. To do this, OnLine must do the following:

1. Write all the pages in the physical log file to disk. After this step, OnLine has effectively restored the OnLine system to the time of the last checkpoint.
2. Apply all the logical log entries put on disk since the last checkpoint. After this step, OnLine will be restored to the last time the logical log buffer was flushed to disk from the log buffer in shared memory.
3. Use the logical log to roll back all uncompleted transactions—that is, transactions that have no logical log entry to COMMIT WORK.

A set of processes (threads in the INFORMIX-OnLine Dynamic Server) called *page cleaners* are responsible for writing modified pages to disk. They write pages to disk either during a checkpoint or, if the buffer cache gets too dirty, between checkpoints.

1.6 CLIENT/SERVER COMMUNICATION

INFORMIX-OnLine Local Communication

When the application process and the INFORMIX-OnLine database server are on the same system, they communicate to each other via the UNIX Inter-Process Communication (IPC) mechanism of unnamed pipes. Pipes are an efficient method of communication between two processes.

INFORMIX-OnLine Dynamic Server Local Communication

The INFORMIX-OnLine Dynamic Server allows local communication by shared memory, streams (starting with version 7.10.UD1), or TCP/IP.

The shared-memory method uses the message segments in shared memory to hold messages sent back and forth from the application and the database server.

TCP/IP uses the TCP/IP protocol to send and receive messages. When the communication is between processes on the same machine, a method of communication called *local loopback* is used. On most machines, this means that the processes do not actually go out across the network to deliver the messages, since the client and server are both on the same machine.

The 6.0 or later application tool (when it is INFORMIX-ESQL/C, INFORMIX-ESQL/COBOL, DB-Access, or INFORMIX-4GL) uses an environment variable, called INFORMIXSERVER, to determine how to connect to an OnLine system. INFORMIX-SERVER is a key into a file called the **sqlhosts** file, which gives more information on how to connect to the OnLine system:

- The host name where the OnLine system is running,
- The type of communication (TCP/IP or shared memory), and
- The port number, if TCP/IP is used.

The **sqlhosts** file is in the directory **$INFORMIXDIR/etc**. For more information about the format of this file, consult your INFORMIX documentation.

Remote Communication

TCP/IP using the TLI or sockets programming interface is usually used to perform client/server communication when the application and the database server reside on different machines.

A version 5.0 application tool cannot communicate directly to the database server across the network. Instead, the communication occurs through an intermediate database server on the client side (see Fig. 1.8). This process is either a relay module or an actual database server that performs only communication tasks.

Figure 1.8-Remote client server communication with a 5.0 tool

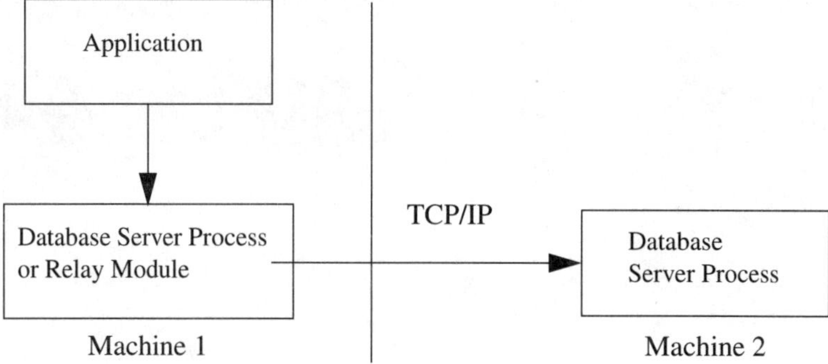

For version 6.0 and later applications, the communication libraries are embedded in the application code, so no additional process is needed on the client system (see Fig. 1.9).

Figure 1.9-Remote client server communication with 6.0 or later tools and the INFORMIX-OnLine Dynamic Server

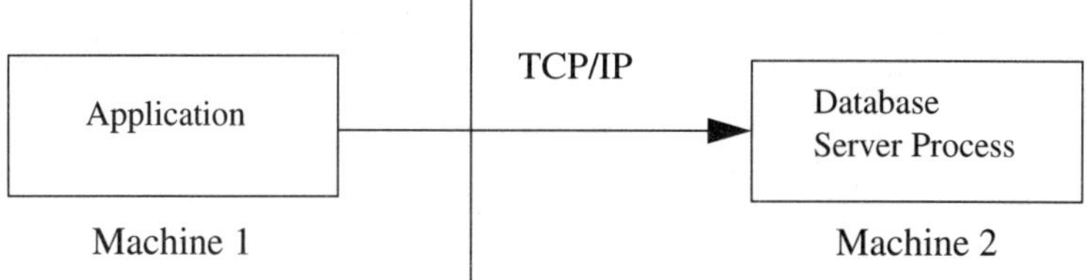

1.7   MULTIPLE ONLINE SYSTEMS

It is possible to have more than one OnLine system on one machine. Each OnLine system is sometimes known as an OnLine instance. An OnLine instance has its own processes, shared memory, and disk. OnLine instances cannot communicate in any way except through the remote client/server communication method, TCP/IP. The shared memory is kept separate by using a different shared memory key.

1.8   FOR MORE INFORMATION

If you are interested in more information about the internal architecture of the OnLine system, refer to the product documentation: *INFORMIX-OnLine Administrator's Guide* or *INFORMIX-OnLine Dynamic Server System Administrator's Guide*.

Chapter 2

Performance Tuning

The world of performance analysis starts in one place: defining the problem to be solved or decision to be made. Tuning configuration parameters or changing database design means nothing unless an issue can be solved by doing it.

This chapter covers the following topics:

- Proactive versus reactive performance considerations
- Determining performance expectations
- How to approach performance issues
- Performance tests
- Performance tools and monitors
- Configuration parameters

2.1 PROACTIVE VERSUS REACTIVE PERFORMANCE CONSIDERATIONS

Performance issues can be divided into two types, proactive and reactive.

Proactive performance issues are those that affect future decisions of an organization. They should surface while planning for a new or revised production environment. They are easier to define and easier to measure. In addition, by pinpointing potential problems during the planning phase, you can set the expectations of management and users of the kind of performance they will experience during a production environment, and you can avoid some of the reactive performance issues that may occur once a system is in place.

Some possible proactive performance issues might be

- Evaluate database design alternatives,

- Evaluate data placement options,

- Check program designs,

- Compare distributed database performance versus nondistributed database performance,

- Compare client/server performance versus single-system performance,

- Evaluate whether the hardware is sufficient to support possible production database activity,

- Determine expected response times in average queries,

- Determine how growth in the size of a table will affect the overall query performance, and

- Test new application tool or database server releases.

Reactive performance issues are usually those that occur after a system is in production, such as

- Complaints from users about response time,

- Unexpectedly lengthy completion time of certain activities (reports, index builds, massive data loads, etc.), and

- Inability to perform tasks in a specific period of time, such as archives and data loads.

Once a reactive performance issue occurs, the cause can be one of a myriad of different possibilities. Also, the amount of time an administrator has to solve a reactive performance issue is usually much less than if problems were found during the design or production planning phase.

2.2 DETERMINING PERFORMANCE EXPECTATIONS

End users usually perceive performance in terms of *response time*. Response time is usually defined as the interval of time between when the user presses the **Execute** or **Return** key on the workstation or terminal and when the information is returned and displayed on the screen.

It is important to determine an acceptable response time for each critical activity and even more important to make sure the performance criteria are written down and agreed to by all parties involved in an application development project.

A common mistake in development projects is to either ignore performance issues altogether in the design document or state performance goals in a vague manner. Here's an example of a vague response-time goal:

All users should get a response back within 3 seconds.

In addition to being unrealistic, this goal is also vague. Do all parties understand what response time is? A 3-second response time severely restricts the application developer to keeping *all* transactions very small in order to meet the response-time goal.

Here's an example of a response-time goal that is a little more realistic and more specific to the application:

> When a user presses the **Execute** key in any screen in the reservation application, the database transaction should be completed and a response returned to the user within 3 seconds 80% of the time and within 6 seconds 20% of the time.

The goal states the application where it is applicable. Some applications can be organized in groups of like database activity, such as table maintenance screens, and can be given the same performance goal. In addition, the goal allows for some slippage during busy periods. A highly utilized disk or processor can severely affect response time.

Another type of measurement that might be important in a system is *throughput*, where a certain amount of activity must be accomplished in a fixed amount of time. This measurement is most important during batch activities, such as reporting and data loading. The system design document should address these requirements as well; for example,

> The mainframe transfer application runs nightly and must load 32,000 rows in the transaction table and 10,000 rows in the contact table. This activity must complete in 5 hours.

After the performance goals are stated in writing and accepted by all parties, it is the administrator's responsibility that those goals be met. Unless you like the idea of telling the application development staff that an application redesign is necessary or of putting in a purchase order for last-minute hardware, *don't wait until the last minute to test out these performance goals in a benchmark environment*!

2.3 HOW TO APPROACH PERFORMANCE ISSUES

1. Define what unit of work you will measure. For example, you may be testing the ability of the hardware to handle 50 users running a certain type of transaction and still maintain the response time specified in the performance goals.

2. Determine how you will measure it. For proper measurement of improvements, you must have two things:

   - *A repeatable test.* Without a repeatable test, there is no way to measure improvements accurately. However, it is just this factor that is missing in most reactive performance situations. Whatever the reason (lack of a proper test environment, lack of time for a proper test, lack of statistics), many times an administrator is forced to make adjustments in tunable parameters and rely solely on the word of a user to judge whether a change was effective. Although measuring activity in the ever-changing production environment is not the best method, sometimes it is the only choice. Thankfully, you can use tools that come with the operating system and with OnLine to determine the effectiveness of many types of parameter changes in the absence of a repeatable test.

- *A reliable measure of true activity.* When choosing a measurement, make sure it approximates true production activity. This means that you will have to reproduce at least a subset of the production system in a test environment. For example, to test response time in a production environment with 50 users, it would be inappropriate to measure response time in a test environment with five users. Although you can attempt to model a larger user population given the results of a small number of users, this technique is risky because of the large number of performance variables that can interfere with performance.

3. Determine the factors that affect the performance issue you are studying. This step is where your knowledge of OnLine, the operating system, and the hardware is most important. This step is what the rest of this book is about. You must understand the relationships that the OnLine configuration parameters have with each other and with the rest of the system.

4. Perform tests. This is where the actual analysis work occurs. It is important here to proceed as you did in school science projects—with a careful and impartial test and good recording of the results. Make sure the test interval is long enough to eliminate the effect of start-up and completion activities. In addition, it is very important to confine the number of variables between tests to one. For example, if you run a test and then change several parameters and rerun the test with better results, which parameter actually helped performance? Ideally, the discipline you should follow is shown in Figure 2.1.

Figure 2.1-The test execution cycle

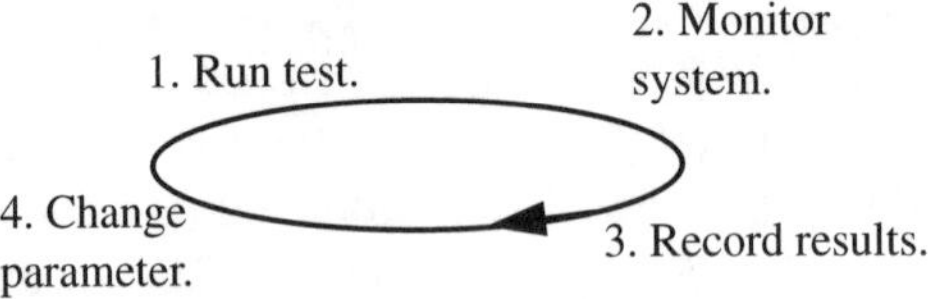

5. Evaluate performance. This step is where you prepare the test results you gathered in the previous step and determine which factors improved or hampered performance. If you are preparing results for management, you must place your conclusions in a well-prepared document.

2.4   PERFORMANCE TESTS: STANDARD TESTS OR CUSTOM TESTS

It is not unusual to spend several weeks writing tests to approximate your production activity, especially in the early stages of a project. Because of the extra time required to write custom tests, some administrators and system evaluators choose to rely on standard tests to approximate performance. The most common tests for evaluating database performance are those specified by the Transaction Processing Council (TPC). The council is one of several organizations formed to develop and control standard benchmarks. The TPC benchmarks are actually a set of specifications for how the standard benchmarks should be run. Normally the hardware vendors create, run, and publish the results of a TPC benchmark, usually in hopes of using their results to win sales. The hardware vendor chooses the DBMS to be used for the benchmark.

The TPC offers specifications for several types of benchmark tests:

- **TPC Benchmark A.** TPC-A is the earliest test specification, introduced in 1989, modeling a banking transaction. A series of simple SQL statements (a few UPDATE statements and an INSERT statement) are executed with a think time to simulate users.

- **TPC Benchmark B.** TPC-B is the same as TPC-A, except that it has no simulated user interaction. Transactions are submitted one after another with no think time.

- **TPC Benchmark C.** TPC-C is a more complex OLTP benchmark specification, which makes it a little more realistic than the TPC-B benchmark. It models an order-entry environment and offers a variety of multirow database operations instead of the same transaction executed repeatedly.

- **TPC Benchmark D** (decision support). TPC-D is a benchmark specification that is geared toward complex queries.

Hardware vendors usually publish a transactions-per-second figure, relating it to a cost of hardware, software, and maintenance. However, there is much more valuable information available in the full disclosure report that is required. You can get the full disclosure from the hardware vendor that conducted the test or from the Transaction Processing Council for a fee.

You can use the TPC benchmarks for several purposes:

- **To evaluate hardware platforms.** For example, if your production system is heavily transaction-oriented, you may examine the TPC-B performance numbers on several hardware platforms in order to choose the best one for your needs.

- **To evaluate hardware upgrades.** If the same hardware vendor has published performance numbers on both the older and newer hardware configurations, you can compare the benchmark results between the two to estimate the amount of increased capacity you can experience in your production system.

- **To evaluate database products.** The major database vendors publish TPC results on the major hardware platforms. Although the benchmark results should not be the only deciding factor in a database purchasing decision, it can be one factor.

Since TPC benchmarks are very generalized, *they should not replace your own custom tests*. Many potential database customers require the database vendor to participate in a custom benchmark test that more completely represents the customer's application and database requirements.

2.5 EVALUATING PERFORMANCE—PERFORMANCE TOOLS AND MONITORS

Even if you are monitoring performance of a database product, you cannot examine its behavior without taking into account the behavior of the operating system and hardware. For example, if database INSERTs are slow, you might examine the disk I/O. Perhaps the disk is handling its capacity, and the data should be spread across multiple disks. As another example, if your system is short on memory, you may see disk access increase as well because pages in memory are written to disk during swapping or paging operations to make room for other pages.

Unfortunately, every UNIX machine varies in what kind of monitoring tools it offers. You should examine your operating system documentation for more information. However, for your information, here is a summary of some tools that are offered on various operating systems and hardware platforms. We will discuss how these tools can be used in various situations throughout the book.

vmstat

The **vmstat** tool reports information on process, memory, CPU, and some disk activity. Besides the command line options, **vmstat** has two parameters that you will almost always include—interval and count. The following example will show intervals of every 2 seconds, ten times:

```
vmstat 2 10
```

The first line in the report shows the activity since the system was last booted. The remaining lines show activity for the interval.

Here is sample output of **vmstat**. The key fields to look at are the user, system, and idle percentages on the right-hand side of the report.

```
%vmstat 2 3
procs       memory                page          disk          faults      cpu
r  b  w  avm  fre   re at pi po fr de sr d0 d1 d2 d3 in  sy  cs  us sy  id
0  0  0  0    2060 0  7  0  0  2  16 0  0  0  0  0  7   75  17  3  1   96
0  0  0  0    2052 0  28 4  0  24 0  9  15 0  0  0  72  269 61  21 8   71
0  0  0  0    2052 1  25 0  0  12 0  5  8  0  0  0  72  256 60  7  8   85
```

iostat

The **iostat** utility provides more information on disk activity. The **iostat** utility works similarly to **vmstat** in that each line represents activity for a time interval. Here is some sample output of **iostat**:

```
% iostat 2 5
tty        dk0              dk1            cpu
tin tout bps tps  msps bps  tps  msps us  ni  sy  id
0   0    3   0    0.0  1    0    0.0  2   0   1   96
0   25   0   0    0.0  0    0    0.0  10  0   1   89
0   25   66  10   0.0  0    0    0.0  23  0   9   68
```

The key fields in this output are the bytes per second value (bps) for each disk listed.

ps

The **ps** command is a powerful tool to get a snapshot of memory and CPU usage at a particular point in time. The **ps** command can differ in format and options, but generally the following information can be listed for each process in the UNIX system:

- The percentage of CPU currently being used,
- The percentage of memory currently being used,
- The amount of memory currently being used,
- The status of the process (running, idle, etc.), and
- The priority of the process ("nice" value).

sar

The **sar** utility lists information about CPU usage, disk usage, and many other interesting facts about a system. Some systems may have the **sar** utility, but not the **vmstat** and **iostat** utilities.

A simple **sar** output that shows CPU usage every 5 seconds follows:

```
%sar 5 5

10:06:22 %usr %sys %wio %idle
10:06:27 34    1    0    65
10:06:32 34    2    0    64
10:06:37 34    1    0    65
10:06:42 17    1    0    82
10:06:47 1     1    0    98
```

Graphical Tools

Some hardware vendors offer more complex performance tools, which can greatly simplify collection and monitoring, especially for multiple systems. Hewlett-Packard offers HP/UX Glance, a very useful graphical performance monitor. A+Performance Management is a tool sold by SunExpress and includes a single collection and access point and a graphical interface.

When using these kind of tools, it is important to remember that they may be using some CPU themselves to run. Some can run the graphical front-end on a different system than they are reporting on. Also, you must make sure that you understand exactly what each graph or report is depicting.

INFORMIX Utilities

INFORMIX offers two utilities helpful to performance tuning: **onstat** and **oncheck** (**tbstat** and **tbcheck** for INFORMIX-OnLine). The **onstat** utility actually reads shared memory for a snapshot of information about the OnLine system. Some of the information that can be obtained in both INFORMIX-OnLine and INFORMIX-OnLine Dynamic Server is listed here.

```
-a print all info
-b print buffers
-c print configuration file
-d print dbspaces and chunks
-h print buffer hash chain info
-k print locks
-l print logging
-m print message log
-p print profile counters
-s print latches
-t print tblspaces
-u print users
-z zero profile counts
-B print all buffers
```

```
-C print btree cleaner requests
-D print dbspaces and detailed chunk stats
-R print LRU queues
-x print transactions
-X print entire list of sharers and waiters for buffers
```

You can reset many of the shared memory counters in these options by running **onstat -z**. This is useful for tuning purposes when you want to measure activity for a certain interval of time. These counters are also reset when the OnLine system is brought down and back up.

INFORMIX-OnLine Dynamic Server also offers a myriad of other parameters that show what is happening in the multithreaded subsystem. Some of these options are interesting but not really useful for tuning.

```
-g xxx (xxx is one of the following options)
all print all MT information
ath print all threads
wai print waiting threads
act print active threads
rea print ready threads
sle print all sleeping threads
spi print spin locks with long spins
sch print VP scheduler statistics
lmx print all locked mutexes
wmx print all mutexes with waiters
con print conditions with waiters
stk <tid> dump the stack of a specified thread
glo print MT global information
mem <pool name|session id> print pool statistics
seg print memory segment statistics
rbm print block map for resident segment
nbm print block map for non-resident segments
afr <pool name|session id> print allocated pool fragments
ffr <pool name|session id> print free pool fragments
ufr <pool name|session id> print pool usage breakdown
iov print disk IO statistics by vp
iof print disk IO statistics by chunk/file
ioq print disk IO statistics by queue
iob print big buffer usage by IO VP class
ppf [<partition number> | 0], print partition profiles
tpf [<tid> | 0], print thread profiles
ntu print net user thread profile information
ntt print net user thread access times
```

```
ntm  print net message information
ntd  print net dispatch information
nss  <session id> print net shared memory status
nsc  <client id> print net shared memory status
nsd  print net shared memory data
sts  print max and current stack sizes
dic  print dictionary cache information
qst  print queue statistics
wst  print thread wait statistics
prc  print procedure cache information
dsc  print data distribution cache information
ses  <session id> print session information
sql  <session id> print sql information
dri  print data replication information
```

When tuning a system, you may want to store **onstat** reports and reports from system utilities in a file. This is a simple (yet important) matter of redirecting the output to a file.

```
onstat -p >> results.out
```

You can also run the **onstat** option every *n* seconds and redirect the output to a file, for example:

```
onstat -r 10 -p >> results.out
```

INFORMIX-OnLine Dynamic Server has the *System Monitoring Interface* (SMI), which can be used to retrieve most of the information that can be gathered with **onstat**. The SQL interface allows you to retrieve the information easily within a program or the DB-Access utility and to display it or store it in a history table.

The SMI "tables" are stored in a database called **sysmaster**, which is created automatically at initialization time or when an INFORMIX-OnLine system is converted to INFORMIX-OnLine Dynamic Server. The SMI tables don't actually contain data; instead, they store a pseudo-table id that is recognized internally by OnLine and used to access the actual data in shared memory.

Although there are quite a few SMI tables, only important tables and views that are supported by INFORMIX are listed here, along with the **onstat** option, which gives similar information:

```
sysdatabases - Databases in the OnLine system
systabnames  - Tables within all databases
syslogs  - Logical log information (onstat -l)
sysdbspaces  - Dbspace information (onstat -d)
syschunks  - Chunk information (onstat -d)
syslocks  - Lock information (onstat -k)
```

```
sysvpprof - Virtual processor information (onstat -g glo)
syssessions - Session information (onstat -g ses)
syssesprof - Session level profile information (onstat -g ses)
sysextents - Extent information
syschkio - I/O statistics by chunk (onstat -D)
sysprofile - System profile information (onstat -p)
sysptprof - Tblspace profile information (onstat -t)
systhreads - Information about threads (onstat -g ath)
sysconfig - Current settings of configuration parameters
     (onstat -c)
syspools - Memory pools (onstat -g mem)
syssegments - Shared memory segments allocated to OnLine
     (onstat -g seg)
syssqexplain - Query path information (same as SET EXPLAIN
     output)
```

You can get a listing of columns for these tables by selecting the **sysmaster** database in the DB-Access utility and choosing the **Table:Info** option.

While **onstat** and SMI principally read statistics found in shared memory, the **oncheck** (**tbcheck** in INFORMIX-OnLine) utility reads information found in disk structures. Although **oncheck** is used mainly for problem diagnosis, a few options are useful for viewing the layout of data on disk. The **oncheck** options are listed next:

```
r - reserved pages (-cr)
e - extents report (-ce)
c - catalog report (-cc)
k - keys in index (-ci)
K - keys and rowids in index (-cI)
l - leaf node keys only (-ci)
L - leaf node keys and rowids (-cI)
d - TBLSpace data rows (-cd)
D - TBLSpace data rows including bitmaps, remainder pages and
     blobs (-cD) t - TBLSpace report
T - TBLSpace disk utilization report
p - dump page for the given [table and rowid | TBLSpace and
     page number] P - dump page for the given chunk number and
     page number
B - BLOBSpace utilization for given table(s)
     [database:[owner.]]table
```

Another way of monitoring activity (not just performance) is to read the OnLine message log. The message log is just a file that stores diagnostic messages about the activity of the OnLine system. **onstat -m** will give the path name and list the last ten lines of the message log.

Some of the messages that can be displayed in the message log are shown in the following example.

```
15:44:20 INFORMIX-OnLine Initialized -- Shared Memory
     Initialized
15:44:20 Physical Recovery Started
15:44:20 Physical Recovery Complete: 0 Pages Restored
15:44:20 Logical Recovery Started
15:44:20 Logical Recovery allocating 10 worker threads
     ('OFF_RECVRY_THREADS').
15:44:25 Logical Recovery Complete
0 Committed, 0 Rolled Back, 0 Open, 0 Bad Locks

15:44:26 Tbconfig parameter BUFFERS modified from 200 to 1000
15:44:26 Tbconfig parameter LRU_MAX_DIRTY modified from 60 to
     95
15:44:26 Tbconfig parameter LRU_MIN_DIRTY modified from 50 to
     85
15:44:26 Quiescent Mode
15:44:26 Checkpoint Completed: duration was 0 seconds
15:44:38 On-Line Mode
15:45:17 Logical Log 7 Complete
15:49:36 Checkpoint Completed: duration was 8 seconds
```

As you can see from this output, OnLine reports any modification of configuration parameters every time it is restarted. You can use this information in your tuning process to detail what changes occurred between tests.

2.6   CONFIGURATION PARAMETERS

The principal method for tuning an OnLine system is through a set of configuration parameters. They are stored in a file under the directory **$INFORMIXDIR/etc**. The file can have an arbitrary name; OnLine finds it through an environment variable you set called ONCONFIG (TBCONFIG for INFORMIX-OnLine). There is one configuration file for every OnLine system or instance running on the machine.

For the most part, the configuration parameters are read once before the OnLine system comes up. Therefore, you can change the configuration parameters anytime while the OnLine system is up, but the new parameters will not take affect until the next time the OnLine system is brought down and back up.

To change configuration parameters, you can either edit the file or use the **onmonitor** (**tbmonitor** in INFORMIX-OnLine) utility, which is a more user-friendly menu interface to the configuration file.

Chapter 3

Database Design

You can tune the hardware, the operating system, and the OnLine system; but if the database is not designed properly, optimal performance is not attainable. This chapter gives an overview of the important performance issues in designing an OnLine database. Some of the database design and implementation issues discussed in this chapter include

- Transaction logging
- Indexing
- Normalization
- VARCHAR columns
- BLOB columns
- Stored procedures and triggers
- INFORMIX-OnLine Dynamic Server database design issues

3.1 TRANSACTION LOGGING

Databases in an OnLine system can have one of three logging options: no logging, unbuffered logging, or buffered logging. The option you choose can affect performance of the database and the OnLine system. A discussion of these options follows.

No Logging

A database with *no logging* means that any Data Manipulation Language (DML) statements, such as INSERT, UPDATE, or DELETE statements, for that database are not recorded in the logical log and cannot be rolled back. The implications of an unlogged database should be understood very clearly should you decide to create one.

- An application connecting to an unlogged database cannot take advantage of the concept of a transaction. A *transaction* is a set of SQL statements that are effectively treated as one operation. If one SQL statement in the transaction fails, all SQL statements in the transaction will be rolled back as if they never happened. Without logging, the BEGIN WORK and COMMIT WORK statements in an application will cause an SQL error to occur.

- If the machine crashes or the OnLine system fails for any reason, what you thought to be completed may not actually have been completed. Without logging, the database will be restored to the time of the last checkpoint (which could be 5–10 minutes before the crash), effectively wiping out all completed operations since that time.

- If, for some reason, you must restore from an archive, no roll forward can occur because the OnLine system has not recorded transactions. You will only be able to recover back to the point of the last archive.

Having said this, it is important to note that a database with no logging performs faster in database update operations than a database that is logged. If your database holds noncritical information or if data can be reloaded from an external source if necessary, then, by all means, don't log the database. For example, a phone company holding switch data that are used for reporting trend information may not care if a portion of the data is lost.

No logging is the default mode when a database is created. To change a database with logging to no logging for INFORMIX-OnLine, run the following command:

```
tbtape -N database_name
```

For INFORMIX-OnLine Dynamic Server, run

```
ontape -N database_name
```

Buffered Logging

For more critical data, you will probably want to turn logging on. The most efficient form of logging is *buffered logging*. With this option, all the database update activity is recorded in the form of transaction entries in the logical log. The *logical log* is an area on disk created and controlled by OnLine specifically for recovery purposes. To cut down on the number of disk writes required to the logical log, the log entries are placed in a memory buffer, called the *logical log buffer*. The default size of this buffer is 32 kbytes, but it is tunable with the LOGBUFF configuration parameter. When the buffer is full, it will be flushed to the logical log file on disk. The logical log buffer is also flushed during a checkpoint.

Because OnLine is writing to disk in 32-kbyte chunks, buffered logging is the most efficient of logging forms. However, there is a drawback. You can lose transactions that you thought were committed if they are in the logical log buffer and the OnLine system or the machine goes down for any reason. In the example in Figure 3.1, the unbuffered logging database will flush the buffer immediately after the INSERT transaction is completed, so no transaction will be lost. However, the buffered logging example shows user 1's transaction completed, but the transaction is not flushed to the logical log on disk immediately. Instead, the transaction is not flushed to disk until the buffer is full. If the OnLine system goes down for any reason, user 1's transaction will not be recovered.

You can specify that a database have buffered logging when you create it using the following syntax:

```
CREATE DATABASE database_name
    WITH BUFFERED LOG
```

You can also change a database from unbuffered logging to buffered logging once the database has been created with the **tbtape** command (for INFORMIX-OnLine Dynamic Server, substitute **tbtape** with **ontape**).

```
tbtape -B database_name
```

If you want to start logging on a database that has no logging, you must initiate an archive at the same time that the logging is changed.

```
tbtape -s -B database_name
```

Unbuffered Logging

The safest yet most inefficient form of logging is unbuffered logging (see Fig. 3.1). Databases with unbuffered logging cause the logical log buffer to be flushed any time a transaction is committed. This could be after one statement, or several in a longer transaction that uses BEGIN WORK and COMMIT WORK. Control is not returned to the user when a transaction is committed until the buffer is written to disk. Unbuffered logging means that you will never lose a committed transaction if the system goes down. It also means that the logical log will be one of the most I/O-intensive areas on disk and that overall performance, especially for smaller transactions, will be affected.

Note that since all databases in an OnLine system share the same logical log buffer, databases with buffered logging will be affected by any database that has unbuffered logging in that the buffer will be flushed every time a transaction commits on the database with unbuffered logging.

You can specify that a database has unbuffered logging when you create it, using the following syntax:

```
CREATE DATABASE database_name
        WITH UNBUFFERED LOG
```

You can also change a database from buffered to unbuffered logging once the database has been created with the **tbtape** command (**ontape** for INFORMIX-OnLine Dynamic Server).

```
tbtape -U database_name
```

If changing from no logging to unbuffered logging, an archive must be performed at the same time that logging is changed.

```
tbtape -s -U database_name
```

Figure 3.1-Buffered versus unbuffered logging

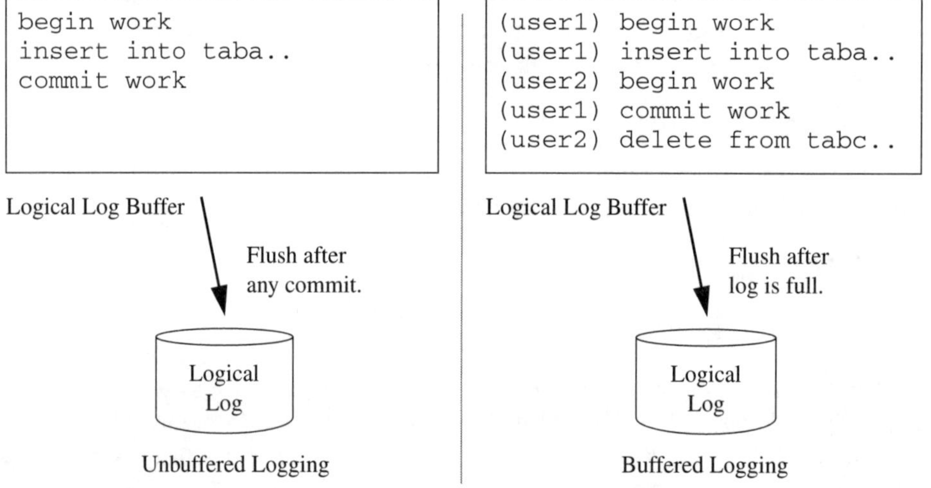

3.2   ANSI DATABASES

An ANSI database complies to ANSI specifications. You specify that a database is ANSI in the CREATE DATABASE statement.

Administrators choose to use an ANSI-compliant database because it conforms to certain standard behaviors. Applications accessing any ANSI database can expect it to act in certain ways. One of the behaviors of an ANSI database is that it must have unbuffered logging. Also, applications are required to be in transaction at all times. BEGIN WORK is implicitly invoked starting when the database is accessed and immediately after a COMMIT WORK is executed in the application. This and other behaviors directly affect locking and, hence, the performance of the database server. For example, read locks (locks held on data that are accessed in a SELECT statement) will be held until the end of the transaction in an ANSI database.

Unless standards are important to your organization and you are willing to compromise performance for those standards, do not create an ANSI database.

3.3 INDEXING

Indexes are used to improve the time it takes to access data in a table. They can affect not only query performance, but performance on UPDATE, INSERT, and DELETE statements as well. To understand the implications that indexes have on performance, it is important to know how they work.

INFORMIX database servers use b+ trees to create the indexes (hereafter referred to as *b-trees*). The special feature of this kind of b-tree is that it is always balanced. In other words, it always takes a set number of index reads to retrieve the data, no matter where the key lies in the b-tree.

A b-tree has a number of levels. The *root*, or *level-0* node, will be the starting point of any user trying to locate a row. The levels under that are *level-1*, *level-2*, and so on. The nodes on the lowest level, or *leaf nodes*, have pointers to the actual data pages that hold the row. Each node is the size of a page.

To find a row, start at the level-0 node and find the key value that is less than or equal to the value for which you are searching. Follow the corresponding pointer to the level-1 node. For each node, repeat the process until you find the leaf node. From the leaf node, you can retrieve the actual address of the data page.

How many levels the b-tree has depends on the number of rows the table has, the size of the index, and how full the b-tree nodes are. Very small tables may have only two b-tree levels. Very large tables may have four or five levels. Every level in the b-tree requires an extra read to get to the data. A b-tree with three levels (as shown in Fig. 3.2) requires three reads to get to the leaf level, and another read is needed to actually get the data. Some of these reads may be from memory because of OnLine's disk caching. However, a large index usually requires one or two disk reads for each random row read.

With a SELECT statement, you will usually be reading only one index for each table. However, with any UPDATE, DELETE, or INSERT statement, all indexes may be read.

- An INSERT statement adds a new row and, consequently, a new entry in the b-tree for every index. If a table has three indexes with three levels each, an INSERT statement will effectively cause nine index reads!

- An UPDATE of a b-tree key effectively consists of a DELETE of the old key and an INSERT of the new key. An UPDATE statement updates only the columns listed in the UPDATE statement. If a column listed in the UPDATE statement has an index, the b-tree for that index will be read. An index b-tree will not be read on columns that are not included in the column list in the UPDATE statement. That's why it's very important to list only the columns you are changing in an UPDATE statement.

- A DELETE statement must read all b-trees to delete the key for each row that will be deleted.

Figure 3.2-An index b-tree

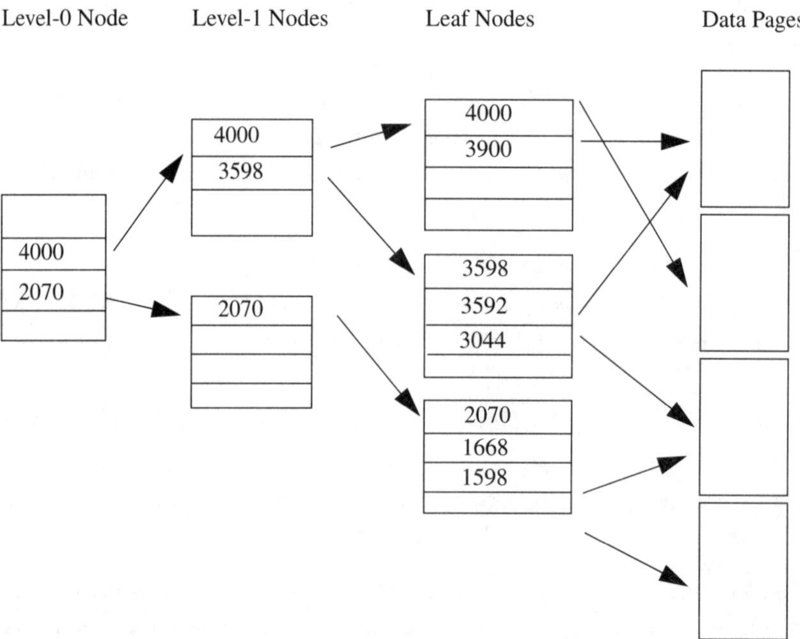

You can see from this discussion that, although indexes may improve query performance, they will affect other SQL operations negatively. You must decide where optimal performance is more important—in query operations or update operations. Most administrators try to strike a balance between the two by creating only the minimal number of indexes on tables that might satisfy the important queries.

3.4   IMPROVING PERFORMANCE WITH INDEXES

Putting indexes on important columns will prevent sequential table reads. Index reads are preferable unless a query reads a large amount of data.

Generally, you will add at least one index for each table, on the primary key. In fact, the PRIMARY KEY designation automatically places an index on the table. For example,

```
CREATE TABLE account(
    account_nbr        SERIAL PRIMARY KEY,
    last_name          CHAR(20),
    first_name         CHAR(20),
     account_balance   MONEY(12,2))
```

This statement automatically creates an index on the account number column.

Another common column to index is any *foreign key*. A foreign key is a column that is used to join one table to another. This type of relationship is also known as *referential integrity*. For example, the **account** table may have a relationship to the **transaction** table, which may have the following schema:

```
CREATE TABLE transaction(
    transaction_id   SERIAL PRIMARY KEY,
    account_nbr      INTEGER REFERENCES
                         account(account_nbr),
    transaction_amt  MONEY(12,2);
```

The REFERENCES keyword specifies that this column is a foreign key. The **transaction** table uses **account_nbr** as a foreign key that relates the transaction table to the primary key, **account_nbr**, in the **account** table. An index is automatically placed on a foreign key column, which will be useful for any query operations that join the two tables.

For more information on the ramifications of using referential integrity, consult your INFORMIX documentation.

Finally, other columns that are commonly used in the WHERE clause of a query (or filter) may be suitable for indexing. You should index columns that can reduce the number of rows in the table that must be read to satisfy the query. However, take care in adding these indexes, as they may cause the same or worse performance in a query. To determine whether an index should be added on a filter column:

1. Before adding the index, run the query or queries that use the filter column and time the duration.
2. Add the index.
3. Run SET EXPLAIN ON, followed by the query. Read the **sqexplain.out** file to determine if the query used the index.
4. Run and time the query to determine if performance is improved by adding the index.

If the query did not use the index, don't bother adding it. If the query used the index and did not increase performance, the index is not useful. Keep the index only if it is used by the query as shown in the **sqexplain.out** file and if performance is improved by the index.

Remember that extra indexes may improve query performance but will cause INSERT, UPDATE, and DELETE performance to degrade slightly.

Once you decide what columns to index, there are some guidelines you can follow to create and monitor indexes.

Monitor Index-Page Fullness

An optimal index for queries would be one that has full b-tree pages. With full pages, one disk read will bring into memory the most key values possible. Also, with full pages, you have no more b-tree levels than absolutely necessary. However, excessive b-tree splits or key deletes may cause index pages to become near-empty. With a sparsely packed index, more disk reads may be required to bring the needed key values into memory.

You can monitor the index-page fullness by running

```
tbcheck -pT database:table
```

Or, for INFORMIX-OnLine Dynamic Server, run

```
oncheck -pT database:table
```

At the bottom of the report, information about each index is listed. For each b-tree level, the number of pages for that level and the average number of free bytes per page are listed. A sample listing for an index follows:

```
Index Usage Report for index iaccount on db:x.account
                      Average   Average
      Level Total    No. Keys  Free Bytes
      ----- --------- --------- ----------
        1     1         4        1973
        2     4         116       506
        3     466       128       217
      ----- --------- --------- ----------
      Total 471        128       223
```

In the preceding example, the leaf pages have an average of 217 free bytes, which means they are approximately 90% full (assuming a 2-kbyte page size). This is a very good average, especially if the table is being updated frequently. If the average free bytes drops below approximately 30–40% of the page size, you might see some improvement by dropping the index with the DROP INDEX statement and re-creating it with CREATE INDEX.

When the index is re-created, INFORMIX-OnLine will try to fill each index page completely (INFORMIX-OnLine Dynamic Server behaves differently, as explained later in this chapter), so you may see a dramatic decrease in the average number of free bytes in the leaf nodes after the index is rebuilt. If the index rebuild caused fewer b-tree levels, you have decreased the number of reads every user must perform for the index by at least one!

Once you rebuild the index, and all pages are full, any new INSERTS will cause a full index page to *split*. This means that one index page will be split into two pages, with each page taking half of the keys of the original page (see Fig. 3.3). After the index is rebuilt, you may see early INSERT performance degradation (because of the high number of splits occurring) and a quick decline in the average fullness of a page. There's not much you can do about this, except to be aware that it will happen and (if feasible) occasionally rebuild the index. In INFORMIX-OnLine Dynamic Server, you can control how much to fill index pages during an index build, as explained later in this chapter.

Figure 3.3-Index pages before and after a split

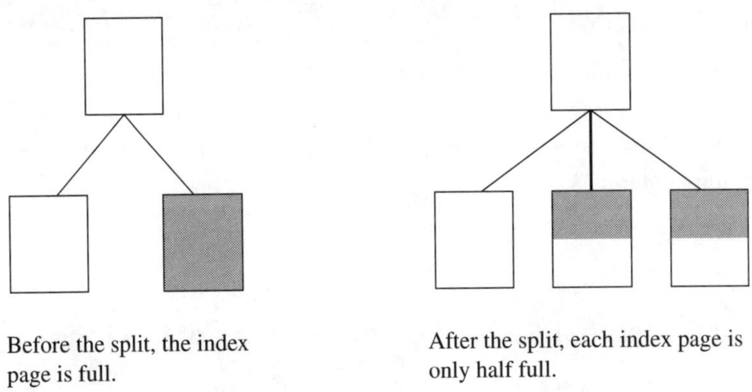

Before the split, the index page is full.

After the split, each index page is only half full.

Keep Key Sizes to a Minimum

By including only the necessary columns in a composite index (an index containing more than one column) and by making sure that the column sizes are not excessive, you can cut down on the key size and therefore put more keys on one page. With more keys on one page, hopefully fewer pages will have to be read from disk.

Avoid Highly Duplicate Indexes

A *highly duplicate index* is one that has a large number of duplicate keys and can severely affect performance for UPDATE and DELETE statements. For example, suppose that you have an index on a **customer_type** column and that there are only five possible

customer_type codes. If the table has one million rows, there could potentially be 200,000 rows with the same type code. The b-tree would store the key value, followed by a list of pointers to each of the physical rows. The problem occurs when you have to DELETE or UPDATE the key value. OnLine must search through the duplicates until it finds the correct key to delete!

To identify highly duplicate indexes, run the following statements on every database:

```
update statistics;
select tabname,idxname,nrows/nunique duplicates
   from systables,sysindexes
   where systables.tabid = sysindexes.tabid
   and systables.tabid >99
```

This SELECT statement will give you an average number of duplicates per key value for each index. To pinpoint a specific highly duplicate value, you will have to examine the contents of the row. Or, with INFORMIX-OnLine Dynamic Server, you can create a distribution on the column with UPDATE STATISTICS and examine the distribution of data values for that column.

To avoid the performance bottleneck of a highly duplicate index, create a composite key with the highly duplicate column and a more unique column. The following example shows the avoidance of a highly duplicate key on **customer_type** by adding the **customer_num** column:

```
CREATE INDEX key_1 on customer
    (customer_type,customer_num)
```

Perform Occasional Checks on the Fitness of the Index

You may want to check that the index is not corrupted, especially if users are complaining about query performance. If an index is corrupted, OnLine will not use it. You can check indexes for each table by running the following **tbcheck** command (**oncheck** for INFORMIX-OnLine Dynamic Server) or dropping and re-creating the index:

```
tbcheck -cI database:table
```

3.5   NORMALIZATION

Database design can fundamentally affect the performance of any application using that database. It is important to design a database thoughtfully so that you can make effective use of SQL in an application.

One of the common methods of grouping data in such a way that it is better suited to the relational model is often referred to as *normalization*. Although it is beyond the scope

of this book to explain normalization, we will discuss when you might want to denormalize a database schema. *Denormalization* is when a table might deliberately break the rules
of normalization to achieve better performance.

A fully normalized database allows for *flexibility*, most specifically in querying for
data. Denormalizing data may make it more difficult to retrieve data cleanly using SQL.

However, a normalized database also tends to be one with a larger number of tables
and rows. Because of that, some database designers tend to denormalize to increase performance in certain circumstances. Some of the more common denormalization strategies
are listed here.

Store Derived Values

A *derived value* is a value that is created by a calculation involving values of other
columns. A common example of a derived value is an account balance. Instead of calculating the account balance by reading all transaction rows for an account, you can keep a running total of the balance.

An example of a normalized version of an **account** and **transaction** table is

```
create table account(
   account_nbr    integer,
   first_name     char(30),
   last_name      char(30));

create table transaction(
   transaction_id  serial,
   account_nbr     integer,
   amount          money(12,2),
   ...
   );
```

To obtain an account balance for an account with the normalized schema, you would
execute an SQL statement such as:

```
select sum(amount) from transaction
   where account_nbr = 22
{Multiple rows must be selected for result}
```

An example of a denormalized version of an **account** and **transaction** table that
stores a derived value is

```
create table account(
   account_nbr    integer,
   first_name     char(30),
```

```
    last_name       char(30),
    balance         money(12,2));

create table transaction(
  transaction_id  serial,
  account_nbr     integer,
  amount          money(12,2),
  ...
  );
```

To obtain an account balance for an account with the denormalized schema, you would execute an SQL statement such as:

```
select balance from account
  where account_nbr = 22;
  {One row is selected for result}
```

One disadvantage of storing derived values is that the balance may get out of sync with the transactions. In our example you can prevent this from happening by using an INSERT, UPDATE, and DELETE trigger on the **transaction** table to update the **account** table automatically. This strategy takes the responsibility away from the programmer to correctly code the update of the **balance** column.

Another disadvantage of storing derived values is that you will have to perform another UPDATE of the derived value table for every change in the dependent table. In our example, for every INSERT of the **transaction** table, one UPDATE of the **balance** column for the **account** table is required.

Store Repeating Groups in One Row

A repeating group is a list of columns within a table that are essentially other instances of the same column. An interesting example of repeating groups is student grades for four grading periods in a year. In a normalized table, each grade would be stored in its own row, so four rows must be selected to get a student's grades for a year. You can denormalize the table by putting all grades in one row, thereby causing a selection of only one row to get the year's grades.

An example of a normalized **grades** table follows:

```
CREATE TABLE grades(
  student_id    INTEGER,
  year          DATETIME YEAR TO YEAR,
  quarter       SMALLINT,
  grade         CHAR(1),
  );
```

To retrieve grades for a student using the normalized table, you would run an SQL statement such as

```
SELECT quarter, grade FROM grades
  WHERE student_id = 33
  ORDER BY quarter;
{Multiple rows are retrieved and must be ordered by quarter}
```

An example of a denormalized **grades** table, with a repeating grades column is

```
CREATE TABLE grades(
  student_id    INTEGER,
  year          DATETIME YEAR TO YEAR,
  quarter1_grade  CHAR(1),
  quarter2_grade  CHAR(1),
  quarter3_grade  CHAR(1),
  quarter4_grade  CHAR(1));
```

To retrieve grades for a student using the normalized table, you would run an SQL statement such as

```
  select quarter1_grade,quarter2_grade,
    quarter3_grade,quarter4_grade
    from grades
    where student_id = 33
{Only one row is retrieved}
```

Although this query might actually run faster with the denormalized table, you should consider other queries that might be executed. For example, finding the average grade for all students is very simple with the normalized table, but much more difficult with the denormalized model.

Split Tables

When separate parts of a table are used by different applications, the table can safely be split into two tables. The advantage of this technique is that the row size for the individual tables is smaller, and more rows can fit on a page.

For example, suppose a table that stores information about hotels in a hotel chain has the following rows:

```
CREATE TABLE hotel(
    hotel_nbr          INTEGER,
    hotel_name         CHAR(30),
    nbr_rooms          SMALLINT,
    hotel_city         CHAR(20),
```

```
        hotel_state          CHAR(2),
        mgr_lname            CHAR(20),
        mgr_fname            CHAR(20),
        hotel_phone          CHAR(12),
        hotel_address        CHAR(80),
        hotel_directions     VARCHAR(60,200));
```

If some information is rarely used in a table, you can split that information into another table. For example, if customers rarely ask for the directions and the address of the hotel, you can split that information into another table.

```
CREATE TABLE hotel(
        hotel_nbr            INTEGER,
        hotel_name           CHAR(30),
        nbr_rooms            SMALLINT,
        hotel_city           CHAR(20),
        hotel_state          CHAR(2),
        mgr_lname            CHAR(20),
        mgr_fname            CHAR(20),
        hotel_phone          CHAR(12),
        );
CREATE TABLE directions(
        hotel_nbr            INTEGER,
        hotel_address        CHAR(80),
        hotel_directions     VARCHAR(60,200));
```

After the split, the row size for the **hotel** table is decreased by potentially 284 bytes. This means that more rows for the **hotel** table can fit on one page, increasing the chances that a needed row will be in memory rather than on disk.

However, if the majority of applications access both tables, this methodology will probably decrease performance, because both tables will have to be accessed.

3.6   HOW TO APPROACH DENORMALIZATION

As you can see from these examples, a sizable risk is involved in denormalizing a database design. It is very important when considering denormalization that you determine how the applications will use the data and whether performance will improve enough to warrant the inconvenience of a denormalized table.

Follow these guidelines when considering denormalizing a database:

1. Determine response time requirements. For example, if users are expecting response times of less than 5 seconds for queries, you may be able to meet that requirement

without denormalizing. Remember that imperceptible performance enhancements won't be recognized and applauded by the user population!

2. Perform a benchmark to determine the performance behavior of a normalized database.

3. Denormalize only if benchmarks do not provide the required response time. Even then, you must also determine how denormalization will affect the response time of the query you are studying, but also *any other operation that will affect the denormalized table.*

Because table denormalization can affect how applications are developed, it is important to make denormalization decisions in advance of the application development stage.

3.7   EFFECTIVE USE OF VARCHAR

Using the VARCHAR character type in some cases may be a great performance enhancement. Some column types have wildly variable sizes. A good example of this is any kind of comments column. You usually make a comments column very large so that it can fit the largest comment. However, some rows will have short comments, and many will have none at all. OnLine always allocates the maximum amount of space for each CHAR column, whether it is used or not, so that when comments are not used, quite a bit of disk space is wasted.

An example of creating a table with a VARCHAR column is

```
CREATE TABLE customer_call(
   customer_id INTEGER,
   date_called DATETIME YEAR TO MINUTE,
   reason_code CHAR(2),
   comments    VARCHAR(10,256));
```

You specify two values when creating a VARCHAR column: the minimum size and the maximum size. The minimum size specifies the minimum number of bytes that will be reserved for the column. The maximum size specifies the largest size the column can reach. If the column is empty, only the minimum number of bytes will be allocated. In the preceding example, only 10 bytes will be reserved for a row with no comments.

Using VARCHAR appropriately will decrease the average row size, allowing more rows to be stored in each data page. The more rows there are per page, the fewer overall disk reads will be required to retrieve the rows.

3.8   EFFECTIVE USE OF BLOB COLUMNS

A *BLOB* (Binary Large OBject) column is used to store unstructured information, such as documents, video, document images, and pictures. There are two types of BLOB columns, BYTE and TEXT. The TEXT column type should be used to store text documents. The BYTE column type should be used to store all other documents with nontext data.

You have two choices as to how to store BLOB columns, in the table or in a separate dbspace called a *blobspace*. The choice you make could have a significant impact on overall OnLine system performance.

BLOB columns stored in the table are actually stored in different pages in the extents where the data pages are held. When a BLOB stored in a table is inserted or updated, it is logged in the logical and physical log, just as regular data are. The BLOB pages are also brought in through the buffer cache. As you can imagine, if the BLOB itself is very large, it strains the logical and physical log resources and causes caching problems in the buffer pool as well.

To create a BLOB stored with the rest of the table, use the IN TABLE keywords in the CREATE TABLE statement; for example,

```
CREATE TABLE document(
  document_id  SERIAL,
  document     BYTE IN TABLE
  );
```

Alternatively, BLOB columns can be stored in a separate blobspace. Not only does the storage location change, but the treatment of the BLOB pages also changes. When this kind of BLOB is inserted or updated, it is not stored in the logical log or physical log, nor is it brought through the buffer pool (other methods are used to ensure recovery in case of a failure).

To create a BLOB column stored in a separate blobspace, include the blobspace name in the CREATE TABLE statement; for example,

```
CREATE TABLE document(
  document_id  SERIAL,
  document     BYTE IN blobsp1
  );
```

Because BLOBs stored in a separate blobspace avoid the standard logging and buffer mechanism, they are an excellent vehicle for large BLOBs. BLOBs that are generally less than a page can safely be stored in the dbspace with the rest of the table.

Another advantage of storing large BLOB columns in a separate blobspace is that the administrator can specify the BLOB page size for each blobspace. By using a larger BLOB page size, large BLOBs can be stored contiguously on disk, rather than in multiple pages in different locations within the extent.

3.9　Stored Procedures and Triggers

Stored procedures are pieces of application code that actually reside in the database. The advantage of stored procedures is that they can cut down on the number of messages passed back and forth between the application process and the database server. Also, the SQL inside a stored procedure is preoptimized, so this step is not required during execution.

A stored procedure has its own overhead, including being read from the database and being converted into an executable format. Because of this overhead, stored procedures do not always enhance performance. Generally, they will improve performance in one or more of these cases:

- The stored procedure contains more than two or three SQL statements. Multiple SQL statements in a stored procedure decrease the amount of message traffic and spread the overhead of a stored procedure over multiple statements.
- The network is slow. If the network is slow, using stored procedures to reduce the amount of message traffic can improve performance.

Triggers are SQL statements that can be executed whenever an INSERT, UPDATE, or DELETE is executed on a certain table. Triggers can effectively improve performance in the same way as stored procedures, especially when they cut down on the number of SQL statements in an application.

3.10　INFORMIX-OnLine Dynamic Server Database Design

There are a few changes in the INFORMIX-OnLine Dynamic Server that may alter the characteristics of a database.

Increased Index Size

The size of the index will probably increase because of the change in index key locking. Each key item uses one extra byte for key value locking. *Key value locking* is a new type of locking where a key value being deleted is not deleted until after the transaction is committed. When you convert a system from INFORMIX-OnLine to INFORMIX-OnLine Dynamic Server, you may see extra pages allocated for each index because of the extra byte allocated per key.

Unfortunately, there is nothing you can do about this increase in size; however, it may be offset by the change in the way index pages are filled when they are created.

FILLFACTOR

When an index is built using INFORMIX-OnLine, the keys are sorted first. This means that most of the pages are filled to 100% capacity, meaning that the b-tree is extremely compact. This is extremely efficient for any query operations using the recently built index, because more keys are packed in one page. However, as soon as an INSERT occurs, there is no room to place the key on the page, and the b-tree page must be split into two pages, each approximately half full. Given enough random INSERTs, the index b-tree can go from being extremely compact to being half full and inefficient. Also, the original INSERT statements can perform poorly because of the extra work required by the server to perform the split.

With INFORMIX-OnLine Dynamic Server, you can specify the amount of space in each index page that will be filled during an index build with a configuration parameter or an addition to the CREATE INDEX syntax. This change will allow you to create an index with room to add key values later, which can minimize the number of index b-tree splits that occur once rows start to be added to the table.

The configuration parameter is called FILLFACTOR. This is the default fill factor of all indexes that are created unless otherwise specified in the CREATE INDEX statement. The following example shows FILLFACTOR set at 90%.

```
FILLFACTOR    90
```

To override the default fill factor for a particular index, specify the FILLFACTOR in the CREATE INDEX statement. The following example will create index pages filled to 100% capacity.

```
CREATE INDEX ix_1 ON customer(customer_num)
FILLFACTOR 100;
```

For static tables, or tables that have only deletions, you should use a FILLFACTOR of 100. Most other tables can use the default FILLFACTOR. There may be some cases where you may want to decrease the FILLFACTOR to 60–70% if the table will be receiving a large number of new rows.

You can monitor the fullness of an index with the **oncheck** command.

```
oncheck -pT database:table
```

The fill factor primarily affects the leaf nodes. The following table was created with 100% fill factor:

```
Index Usage Report for index icustomer on db1.customer
                      Average    Average
     Level    Total   No. Keys   Free Bytes

     -----    -------  ---------  -----------
     1        1        3          1986
     2        3        139        214
     3        417      143        5

     -----    -------  ---------  -----------
     Total    421      143        11
```

Note that the leaf nodes have an average of five free bytes.

You can use this output to adjust the fill factor. Run and save the output of the **oncheck** command after the index is built. After a period of activity, run **oncheck** again and check the average free bytes and total number of index pages. If the average percentage of free bytes is low (how low depends upon your activity, but generally 50% is a good number to start with), you can try decreasing the FILLFACTOR value and re-create the index.

Remember that once an index is created, the fill factor is no longer in effect. Eventually, as INSERTS occur, index pages will fill and begin to split. The fill factor is effective for only a limited period of time.

3.11 DATABASE CONFIGURATION CHECKLIST

Table 3.1 summarizes the important performance aspects of creating and managing a database.

Table 3.1–Database configuration checklist

What to Check	How to Check	How to Alter
Database logging	onmonitor—the **Status:Database** option	**tbtape (ontape)** or by dropping and re-creating the database with a different logging option
Index page fullness	**oncheck -pT** *database:table*	DROP INDEX and CREATE INDEX
Minimum key size	**dbschema -d** *database*	ALTER TABLE to change the column size; DROP INDEX and CREATE INDEX to change a composite key
Highly duplicate keys	Examine the **nunique** column in **systables** or the contents of each row	DROP INDEX and CREATE INDEX using a more unique key (perhaps through a composite key)

Table 3.1–Database configuration checklist (Continued)

What to Check	How to Check	How to Alter
Fitness of an index	**oncheck -cI** *database:table*	**oncheck** or DROP INDEX and CREATE INDEX
Effective use of VARCHAR	Examine contents of large character columns	ALTER TABLE
BLOB column (large BLOBs stored in separate blobspaces)	**dbschema -d** *database*	ALTER TABLE
FILLFACTOR (INFORMIX-OnLine Dynamic Server)	N/A	Alter FILLFACTOR configuration parameter or DROP INDEX and CREATE INDEX with new fill factor

Chapter 4

Disk Performance

Disk reads and writes are two of the highest-cost operations in any computer system. They are also an inevitable part of a database management system. Your goals to improve disk performance should be twofold. First, try to avoid or curtail these operations as much as possible; second, if the I/O is necessary, try to spread the work evenly across disks and over time.

Some of the topics that are discussed in this chapter include

- Disk and memory reads
- Monitoring and tuning the read cache rate
- Monitoring and tuning disk writes
- Monitoring LRU queues
- Disk arrangement considerations
- Disk issues with the INFORMIX-OnLine Dynamic Server

4.1   DISK AND MEMORY READS

OnLine reads database information in units of pages, either 2 or 4 kbytes, depending upon the hardware platform. Reads can occur not only for database SELECTs, but also for any UPDATE and DELETE—OnLine must read the page with the data before it can be deleted or updated.

If the needed page is in the shared memory buffer cache, it will be read from memory. If it is not in memory, the page is read from disk and put in the shared memory buffer cache. Since the buffer cache is shared, many users can access the same page in memory without having to perform a disk read. The more often data are read from memory and not disk, the higher the read "cache" rate. Systems with a high cache rate are obviously more desirable.

4.2   MONITORING READ CACHE RATE

You can monitor the read cache rate by running **onstat -p** (**tbstat -p** for INFORMIX-OnLine Dynamic Server). The first **%cached** field shows the read cache rate since the OnLine system was brought up or since the statistics were cleared with **onstat -z**. In the example excerpt from the following **-p** report, the read cache rate is 99.48%, a very good percentage.

```
Profile
dskreads pagereads bufreads %cached dskwrits pagwrits bufwrits %cached
2383      2389       453962   99.48   14776    20943    77792    81.01
```

The cache rate is calculated for you in this report, but you can calculate the read cache rate yourself by using the following formula:

```
100 * (bufreads - dskreads) / bufreads
```

The read cache rate can vary dramatically, depending upon the applications and the type and size of the data being operated on. If users are accessing the same data constantly, the read cache rate can potentially be very high. If data access is very random and the database is large, the read cache rate might be lower, say, in the 70–80 percentile.

However, there are some steps you can take to make sure the read cache rate is optimal for your OnLine system.

4.3   TUNING READ CACHE RATE

You tune the cache rate primarily by decreasing or increasing the number of shared memory buffers allocated to the buffer cache, with the BUFFERS configuration parameter. By increasing the buffer cache, you allow more pages to stay in memory. Why not add the highest amount of buffers allowed? Because each buffer takes up space in memory—either 2 or 4 kbytes. The page size is set internally and cannot be changed by the administrator. This means that each buffer takes up at least 2 or 4 kbytes of memory. Although a database entirely in memory would get great performance, this probably won't be possible on average size systems if your database is larger than 30 or 40 Mbytes.

The best you can do is to increase the number of buffers until your read cache rate stops increasing dramatically, or you reach the memory constraints of your system. We will be discussing memory issues in chapter 5, but for now, let's concentrate on the buffer cache. To tune the cache rate, follow these steps.

1.   Reset the statistics with **onstat -z**.

2.   Run several hours or days of typical live production. Tuning cache rate during live production is preferable since it is hard to simulate production data access in a benchmark test.

3.   Record the cache rate in percentage from **onstat -p**.

4.   Increase the buffers configuration parameter and bring the OnLine system down and back up.

5.   Repeat steps 2–4 until there is no increase in the read cache rate.

4.4   DISK AND MEMORY WRITES

The INFORMIX-OnLine system has a set of processes, called *page cleaners*, that are responsible for writing pages from the buffer cache to disk. The INFORMIX-OnLine Dynamic Server page cleaners are threads, and they pass the buffer write requests to the AIO subsystem. Page cleaners do this work either during a checkpoint or between checkpoints if the buffer cache gets too full of dirty pages (pages that have been changed since they were read from disk).

The buffer pages are organized into a set of linked lists, called least recently used (LRU) queues (see Fig. 4.1). Each queue is subdivided into a clean queue and a dirty queue. Pages in the clean queue can be overwritten by other users. Pages in the dirty queue must be written to disk before they can be reused. When a database server process needs to read a page from disk, it finds a buffer from the least recently used end of the clean LRU queue and replaces its contents with the contents of the page read from disk. The buffer is then put on the most recently used end of the LRU queue. This mechanism is useful to keep the pages that are used quite often from being overwritten by new pages read from disk.

Figure 4.1-LRU queue

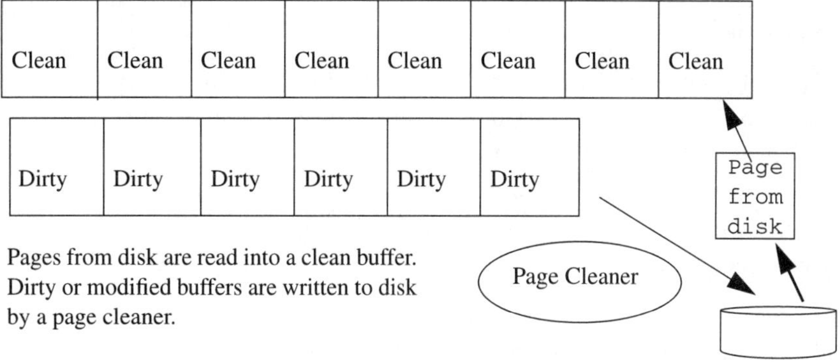

Pages from disk are read into a clean buffer. Dirty or modified buffers are written to disk by a page cleaner.

When a page is written to in memory, it is marked as dirty, meaning its contents have been changed and it must eventually be written to disk. During a checkpoint, which is nothing more than a synchronization between what is in memory and what is on disk, all dirty pages will be read from memory to their respective location on disk.

Between checkpoints, OnLine needs to guard against all the buffers becoming dirty. (When a buffer is dirty, it cannot be written to again until the contents are flushed to disk.) Occasionally, the LRU queues are examined for dirty pages. If a certain percentage of pages within the LRU queue are dirty, the page cleaner will write the dirty pages to disk.

From this discussion you can see that there are two times that pages can be written to disk: *during a checkpoint* and *between checkpoints*. The ideal situation is that we would never write to disk. If we could always perform database operations in memory, we would have 100% cache rate and the best performance. Two things stop us from doing so: the database is probably larger than the buffer cache, and recovery would take a long time if the system crashed.

You could tune the OnLine system to have it write most, if not all, dirty pages to disk only during the checkpoints. This might increase the cache rate somewhat, as you are giving database server processes time to potentially write to a page in memory more than once. If a page is modified in memory more than once, the overall cache rate will improve and, potentially, the overall OnLine system performance will improve too. The problem with this is in the way a checkpoint occurs. When a checkpoint begins, all database server processes are prevented from entering "critical sections" of code, which means that they must wait to do some things, such as writing to pages. If the checkpoint duration is long, this could have some serious implications on performance.

So when might you want to write to disk between checkpoints? There are some valid situations. If the buffer cache cannot hold all the pages that will be altered between checkpoints, some writing must take place. Also, since a checkpoint stops all writes from occurring until the checkpoint is completed, you might see some delay in processing during a checkpoint if there are a large number of dirty pages that must be written.

Figure 4.2(a) shows the performance of a system that relies on most disk writes to occur during a checkpoint. The disk devices will show a spike in activity during a checkpoint and erratic activity between checkpoints. Figure 4.2(b) shows the possible performance of a system that relies on a mixture of disk writes during a checkpoint and between checkpoints. Although there is still some spike of activity during checkpoints, the overall disk activity is more stable and spread more evenly throughout processing.

By spreading out disk activity between checkpoints, you may see a more even response time for users. You may even see better throughput because the shorter check-

Figure 4.2-Disk activity (a) without writes between checkpoints and (b) with writes between checkpoints

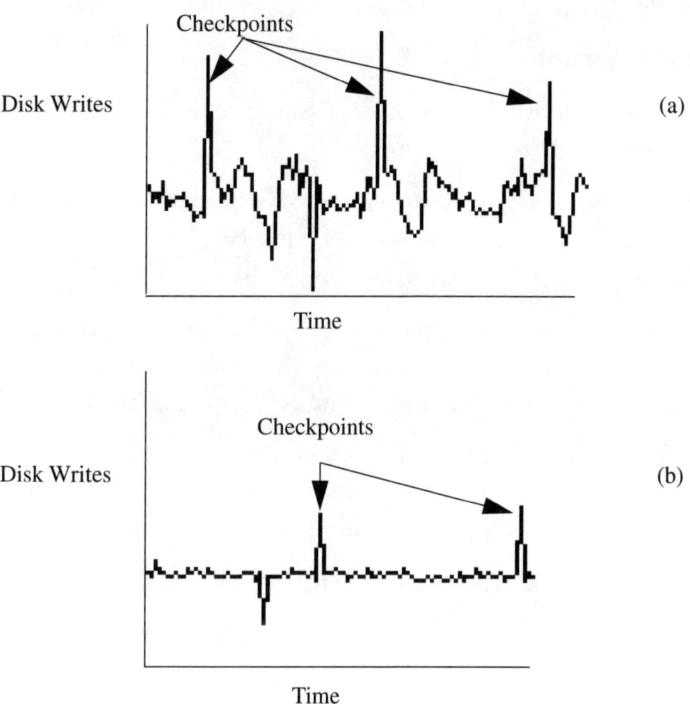

points will not delay transaction activity. However, the write cache rate may decrease somewhat, since OnLine may be writing pages more often to disk. Consider a page that is updated five times in memory between two checkpoints. Using the formula shown previously, you can calculate the write cache rate for the one page as

```
100 * (5 - 1) / 5 = 80%
```

If the page is written to disk once between checkpoints (and once during a checkpoint), the cache rate becomes

```
100 * (5 - 2) / 5 = 60%
```

If the reality in your system is that pages are written many times during a checkpoint, it may be better to perform most disk writes at checkpoint time. If the writes are more random across a larger number of pages, it is best to spread the disk writes evenly between and during checkpoints. Most larger databases fit the latter category.

4.5   TUNING DISK WRITES

You have a great deal of control, through a series of configuration parameters, over how and when pages get written to disk. These configuration parameters are explained next.

Checkpoint Interval

The *checkpoint interval* is the number of seconds between checkpoints. There are several ways to tune the checkpoint interval.

- The CKPTINTVL configuration parameter sets the default interval. Set this to the maximum number of seconds between checkpoints.
- A checkpoint will also occur when the physical log is 75% full.

You can determine the frequency of checkpoints by running **onstat -m**. The **-m** option lists the last few lines of the message log. To view more lines of the message log, you can edit the message log itself (the path name is listed in the report heading).

Every time a checkpoint occurs, a line is written to the message log with the time the checkpoint occurred. You can calculate the approximate interval between checkpoints by subtracting the time of one checkpoint from the time of the previous checkpoint.

Here is an excerpt of sample output from the message log.

```
Message Log File: /home/informix/5.00/online.log
15:49:36 Checkpoint Completed
15:54:48 Checkpoint Completed
```

In this example (although you should check more than one interval), the checkpoint frequency is about 5 minutes.

Instead of setting the checkpoint interval by the CKPTINTVL, consider driving the checkpoint interval by the physical log size. For example, you can set CKPTINTVL to a large number, say, 15 minutes, and set the physical log file to cause a checkpoint to occur every 10 minutes with average activity. This strategy causes checkpoints to occur when there has been sufficient database activity, *not* at a certain time interval.

You can check the current log size by looking at the PHYSFILE configuration parameter. You can increase the physical log size by running the **onparams** utility or changing the size interactively with the **onmonitor** utility.

```
onparams -p -s log-size
```

A large checkpoint interval may make the process of recovery longer. If the OnLine system goes down for any reason, all pages in the physical log must be reapplied. With a large physical log, this may take anywhere from several seconds to 20 minutes, depending upon the physical log size. Start with the checkpoint interval as high as possible without making the recovery process too long, usually somewhere between 5 and 15 minutes. There is no good way to estimate how long recovery will take given a checkpoint interval. The estimation varies between hardware platforms and the number of transactions that must be rolled forward.

LRU Queues

The number of LRU queues can be configured. Since each user can access an LRU queue to read a page or move it within the queue, it is important to configure enough LRU queues to decrease contention for the queues by users and page cleaners. Generally, the number of LRU queues you have will not have a great effect on performance, unless you have configured too few.

Setting LRUs in INFORMIX-OnLine

You can set the number of LRU queues the buffers are assigned to by the LRU's configuration parameter. Only one database server process at a time can alter an LRU queue. If you set the LRU's parameter too small, the database server processes will compete for the LRU queue. If you set the LRU's parameter too high, it will require more internal administrative work to keep track of a large number of queues. A rule of thumb is to configure LRUs to 3 + the number of processors in your system. With more processors, more database server processes can be accessing the LRU queues at once.

Setting LRUs in INFORMIX-OnLine Dynamic Server

The LRU queues are accessed only by threads running within the CPU virtual processors. This means that the amount of contention on LRU queues depends on how many CPU vps are configured (how to configure CPU vps will be discussed in chapter 6). Generally, you want to configure as many LRU queues as CPU vps, starting with at least four.

Page Cleaners

The page cleaner processes in INFORMIX-OnLine are responsible for writing pages to disk. In INFORMIX-OnLine Dynamic Server, the page cleaner threads are responsible for gathering modified pages and submitting the write request to the AIO subsystem.

During a checkpoint, each page cleaner is assigned one or more chunks. The pages are first sorted by chunk and the location within the chunk. Then they are written. Between checkpoints, the page cleaners are assigned to LRU queues, and the page cleaners write out the dirty pages in random order from the LRU queue (see Fig. 4.3).

Figure 4.3-Page cleaners and checkpoints

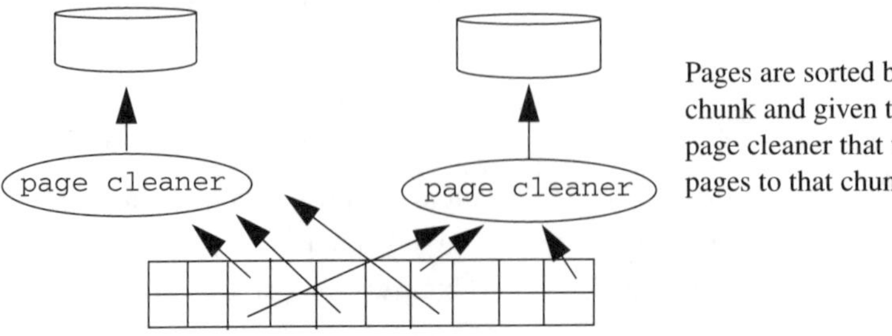

Setting CLEANERS in INFORMIX-OnLine

How you set the number of page cleaners (CLEANERS configuration parameter) depends upon two things: the number of disks and the number of LRU queues allocated. During a checkpoint, it is best to have approximately the same number of page cleaners as disks. The number of page cleaners determines the degree of parallelism during checkpoint writes. If CLEANERS is set to five, the number of disks that can be written to simultaneously is five.

An important thing to remember is that the OnLine system does not know if you have two chunks on the same disk. It will assign chunks to page cleaners in a round-robin fashion. The first chunk that was created goes to page cleaner 1, the second chunk to page cleaner 2, and so on. This means that you should pay special care to how chunks are created at initialization time. For example, if the OnLine system has three disks with two chunks each, you should create chunk 1 on disk 1 first, chunk 2 on disk 2 second, chunk 3 on disk 3 next, chunk 4 on disk 1 next, and so on. With this scheme, each page cleaner would most likely be cleaning a separate disk rather than having two or more page cleaners writing to the same disk at once while other disks remain idle.

The optimal number of page cleaners for writes between checkpoints is somewhat different, however. You should have approximately the same number of page cleaners as you have LRU queues (see the following section for information about setting the number of LRU queues). This is because a page cleaner is assigned at any one time to clean an LRU queue. Having more page cleaners than LRU queues is probably overkill.

Given these two different guidelines for setting page cleaners, which one should you pick? If the majority of disk writes occur between checkpoints, configure the number of page cleaners using the second method (CLEANERS = LRU queues). If the majority of disk writes occur at checkpoint time, configure the number of page cleaners using the first method (CLEANERS = disks). You may then increase or decrease the number of page cleaners slightly to see if it improves performance.

CLEANERS in INFORMIX-OnLine Dynamic Server

With INFORMIX-OnLine Dynamic Server, there is less contention for the LRU queues because the number of processes reading the queues is constrained by the number of CPU vps. As a general guideline, set CLEANERS to the number of disks that will be updated during a checkpoint.

4.6 LRU CONFIGURATION PARAMETERS

There are other configuration parameters used to determine when and how many writes occur between checkpoints. LRU_MAX_DIRTY is the maximum number of pages that must become dirty before the page cleaners start to clean. The LRU_MIN_DIRTY parameter is the percentage of the queue that the page cleaner will leave dirty.

As an example, if LRU_MAX_DIRTY is set to 80 and LRU_MIN_DIRTY to 60, the page cleaners would wake up when 80% of the queue consists of dirty pages. The page cleaners would write dirty pages to disk until only 60% of the pages are full, as shown in Figure 4.4.

Figure 4.4-LRU_MAX_DIRTY and LRU_MIN_DIRTY example

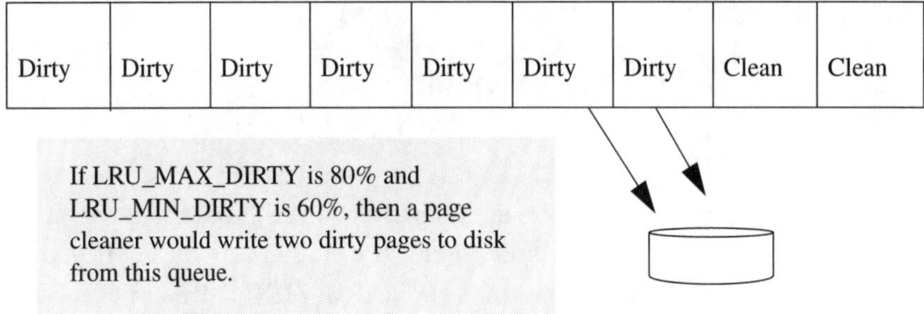

One of the things that the LRU parameters affect is the *checkpoint duration*, the time it takes to complete a checkpoint. It is difficult to determine the checkpoint duration in the INFORMIX-OnLine server. However, you can run **tbstat -r 2**, which will print the status line every 2 seconds, and wait for the CKPT designation to appear in parentheses after the mode. When the CKPT designation disappears (or when the checkpoint message is written to the log), the checkpoint is complete.

In INFORMX-OnLine Dynamic Server, you can determine accurately how long a checkpoint lasted with the **onstat -m** option or by editing the message log. The checkpoint duration is listed next to each checkpoint log entry; for example,

```
16:44:50 Checkpoint Completed: duration was 7 seconds
16:49:55 Checkpoint Completed: duration was 3 seconds
16:54:44 Checkpoint Completed: duration was 0 seconds
```

If checkpoint durations are long, you may try to decrease them by decreasing the LRU_MAX_DIRTY and LRU_MIN_DIRTY parameters so that more pages are written between checkpoints.

To minimize the checkpoint duration, set LRU_MIN_DIRTY and LRU_MAX_DIRTY to small values, such as 5 and 10. This setting would keep the page cleaners working most of the time between checkpoints. Hopefully, by the time the checkpoint occurs, most of the pages are clean.

If you prefer to have most of the disk writes occur during the checkpoint, set LRU_MIN_DIRTY and LRU_MAX_DIRTY to larger values, such as 90 and 98.

Monitoring LRU Queues in INFORMIX-OnLine

You can monitor the LRU queues with the **tbstat -R** command. A sample of the relevant part of the output follows:

```
4 buffer   LRU queues
LRU 0:     8   (40%) modified of 20 total
LRU 1:     4   (26.7%) modified of 15 total
LRU 2:     5   (26.3%) modified of 19 total
LRU 3:     7   (36.8%) modified of 19 total
24 dirty, 73 queued, 75 total, 32 hash buckets, 2048 buffer size
start clean at 60%, stop at 50%
```

From this output you can see that there are four LRU queues (LRUs set to 4). Between checkpoints, page cleaning will start when the queue has 60% dirty buffers (LRU_MAX_DIRTY = 60) and will stop at 50% (LRU_MIN_DIRTY = 50). During a checkpoint, all pages will be cleaned.

The number in parentheses is the percentage of the queue that is dirty. You can see this number rise as pages are written to in memory by database server processes and fall as pages are written to disk by page cleaner processes.

Another interesting command is **tbstat -F**. The output of this command can be used to determine how many writes occurred during checkpoints and how many writes occurred between checkpoints. An example of the interesting part of **tbstat -F** follows:

```
Fg Writes     LRU Writes     Idle Writes     Chunk Writes
31            212            18891           341
```

The **Fg Writes** column specifies the number of writes that occurred because the database server process failed to find a clean buffer to read a page into and, consequently, wrote a dirty buffer to disk itself. This type of write is very inefficient, as the user will be delayed while the database server process performs the write.

LRU Writes are writes that generally occur when the database server process relocates a page on the LRU queue and notices that the percentage of dirty pages exceeds LRU_MAX_DIRTY. Also, after 16 fg writes have been performed, the master daemon will cause the page cleaners to wake up and clean the queues. These writes are classified as LRU writes as well.

Idle Writes are any writes that occur during normal page cleaner activity between checkpoints.

Chunk Writes are the writes performed by page cleaners during checkpoints.

In the sample **tbstat -F** output, most of the disk writes (18,891) occurred between checkpoints.

If you want to perform most writes between checkpoints, you should try to decrease the chunk writes and the fg writes and increase the idle writes and LRU writes. You can cause this to occur by decreasing the LRU_MAX_DIRTY and LRU_MIN_DIRTY parameters.

Monitoring LRU Queues with INFORMIX-OnLine Dynamic Server

You can monitor the LRU queues with the **onstat -R** command. A sample of the relevant part of the output follows:

```
8 buffer LRU queue pairs

#  f/m    length    % of pair    total
0  f      29        58.0%        50
1  m      21        42.0%
2  f      38        76.0%        50
3  m      12        24.0%
4  f      17        34.7%        49
5  m      32        65.3%
6  f      34        68.0%        50
7  m      16        32.0%
8  f      23        43.4%        53
9  m      30        56.6%
10 f      0         0.0%         50
```

```
11 m     50          100.0%
12 f     27          57.4%          47
13 m     20          42.6%
14 F     44          88.0%          50
15 m      6          12.0%
187 dirty, 399 queued, 400 total, 512 hash buckets, 2048 buffer size
start clean at 70% (of pair total) dirty, or 5 buffs dirty, stop at 60%
```

Each line in this output represents either the free buffers or the modified (dirty) buffers in a queue. The **length** is the number of buffers, and the **% of pair** is the percentage of the LRU pair that is either clean or dirty.

From this output you can see that there are eight LRU queues (LRUs set to 8). Between checkpoints, page cleaning will start when the queue has 70% dirty buffers (LRU_MAX_DIRTY = 70) and will stop at 60% (LRU_MIN_DIRTY = 60). During a checkpoint, all pages will be cleaned. In the first queue pair, 58% of the buffers (29) are free, and 42% of the buffers (21) are dirty. You can see the percentage of modified or dirty buffers rise as pages are written to in memory by the session threads and fall as pages are written to disk by the AIO subsystem.

The **onstat -F** command can be used to determine how many writes occurred during checkpoints and how many writes occurred between checkpoints. An example of the interesting part of **tbstat -F** follows:

```
Fg Writes    LRU Writes    Chunk Writes
0            38226         3030
```

The **Fg Writes** column specifies the number of writes that occurred because a session failed to find a clean buffer to read a page into and, consequently, submitted a request to write a dirty buffer to disk itself. This type of write is very inefficient, as the user will be delayed while the AIO subsystem performs the write.

LRU Writes are writes that generally occur when the percentage of dirty pages on a queue exceeds LRU_MAX_DIRTY between checkpoints. Also, after 16 fg writes have been performed, the page cleaners wake up and clean the queues. These writes are classified as LRU writes as well.

Chunk Writes are the writes performed by page cleaners during checkpoints.

In the sample **onstat -F** output, most of the disk writes (38,226) occurred between checkpoints.

If you want to perform most writes between checkpoints, you should try to decrease the chunk writes and the fg writes and increase the LRU writes. You can cause this to occur by decreasing the LRU_MAX_DIRTY and LRU_MIN_DIRTY parameters.

Buffer Pool Size

The buffer pool size is the number of pages from disk that can be put in shared memory. The BUFFERS configuration parameter specifies the number of pages in the buffer pool. This parameter will affect your write cache rate, the percentage of time data are written to memory rather than to disk. It will also affect the LRU configuration. As you increase the size of the buffer pool, more pages will be assigned to each LRU queue. For example, if BUFFERS is set to 1000 and LRUS is set to 10, each LRU queue will handle 100 pages. If LRU_MAX_DIRTY is set to 80%, page cleaning will start when 20 pages have been modified. However, if you increase the buffer pool size to 2000, each LRU queue will handle 200 pages, and page cleaning will start when 40 pages are dirty.

You monitor the write cache rate in the same way as the read cache rate, with **onstat -p**. In the following example report, the write cache rate is 81.01%. As does the read cache rate, the write cache rate varies depending on the applications and the type and size of the data being operated on.

```
Profile
dskreads  pagereads  bufreads  %cached  dskwrits  pagwrits  bufwrits  %cached
2383      2389       453962    99.48    14776     20943     77792     81.01
```

4.7 DISK ARRANGEMENT CONSIDERATIONS

The previous discussion centered on how to alter the operation of OnLine once the system is initialized and the disk layout was set. Additionally, you should consider the placement of tables and other OnLine structures on disk. If disk arrangement is poor, some disks may be overly busy, while others may remain idle. Your OnLine performance will suffer as a result. Ideally, you want to spread the workload evenly across disks.

4.8 HARDWARE ISSUES

There are two issues in disk throughput. One is how fast data can be read from and written to disk. The other is how much data can be written to disk during a certain period of time. The I/O speed depends on the seek time, rotational speed, and transfer rate of the disk itself. Obviously, a faster disk will perform better when a process is reading and writing a large amount of data. When there are many users accessing data, more disks are generally better. However, disk controllers can be a bottleneck if they control access to multiple disks. Discuss with your hardware vendor the best mix of disks to disk controllers.

Some disks support transparent disk striping. The effect of striping can be a chunk that actually spans disks in relatively small pieces. OnLine will support this kind of disk as long as the disk striping is completely transparent to a UNIX read() and write() call. They can be very effective in dividing a large table across disks. You may see a performance gain with disk striping during sequential read operations or when many users are using the same chunk. However, as a note of caution, don't run out and buy a disk like this if you are planning to migrate to later versions of OnLine that support disk fragmentation. Disk striping may actually hurt performance in later versions of OnLine if you use the disk fragmentation feature.

4.9   OTHER DISK USAGE

Before planning disk layout for OnLine data, consider the other disk activity in your system. One important segment of disk for all systems is the swap area, the pages in memory that get copied out to disk. In most cases, the swap area should be on the faster disks and, if possible, spread across multiple disks. For very busy systems, the disks containing swap space will be very busy as well.

If there is any other disk activity on your system, you should isolate the disks that contain the busy file systems, if possible.

4.10   RAW DEVICE OR FILE SYSTEM?

INFORMIX recommends that you use raw devices for your chunk. The recommendation is for two reasons. First, the OnLine data are not subject to the levels of indirection a highly fragmented file system may encounter. With high levels of indirection, the data for a table may reside on different places on a disk, and your performance will suffer on sequential reads. Second, the file system contains its own buffering mechanism, which can be good for many applications, but not necessarily for database applications. When OnLine gets a return value from a write call, it expects the data to be on disk. With buffering on file systems, the page may still be in a memory buffer somewhere, not on disk. Having said that, there are two points to mention. The first point is that some operating systems support a synchronous write call (with the O_SYNC flag), and OnLine will most likely use that if it is present in your system. The second point is that you may actually get better performance with the file system (assuming a minimum of file system indirection) because of the very efficient read-ahead capabilities that some systems have.

The safest alternative, and one that will provide generally good performance in all cases, is to use raw devices.

4.11   PLACEMENT OF ONLINE OBJECTS ON DISK

Here are some factors you need to minimize when choosing the layout of your dbspaces:

- The amount of time it takes for the disk head to reach the data, often called *seek time*;

- Access to the disk by multiple requestors, or *disk contention*; and

- Which disks the controller accesses, or disk *controller contention*.

As a general rule, you want to decrease the seek time for data that is accessed more often. How do you do this? When you choose the center tracks on a disk, the disk head will not have to travel very far in either direction to get to these tracks (see Fig. 4.5). When a disk is partitioned, you specify a set of cylinder numbers for each device. The cylinder numbers in the middle of the range usually denote the center tracks. A device using these cylinder numbers should be reserved for high-priority disk access.

Figure 4.5-The center tracks on disk

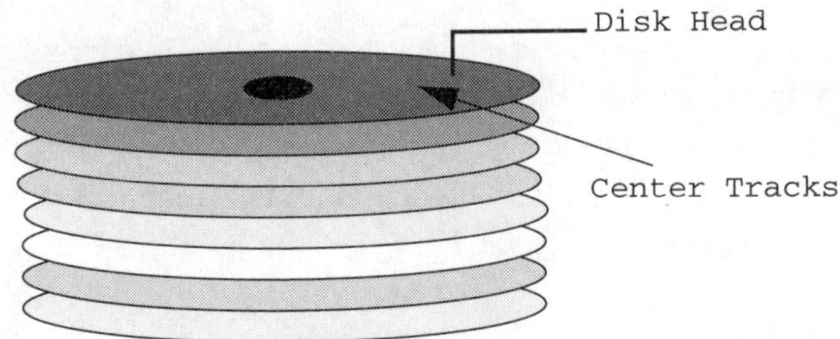

The second factor, disk contention, means that multiple processes are trying to access the same disk at one time. Only one request can be completed at a time per disk, so the other requestors must wait. To cut down on disk contention, you can spread the data that OnLine must access across several disks.

The third factor is the disk controller contention. In many systems, one disk controller can service the requests for multiple disks. In addition to cutting down on disk contention, you need to minimize disk controller contention. Find out which disks are serviced by each controller, and keep that in mind when spreading data across disks.

Physical and Logical Logs

For applications where there is a great deal of data being updated, the physical and logical log placement is important. For decision support applications, the physical and logical logs can take lower priority in disk placement. Why are the physical and logical logs so important? For every write, an entry goes in the logical log buffer. The logical log buffer gets flushed to disk:

- When it is full.

- For databases created with unbuffered logging, when a transaction is committed. It is very important that these writes occur quickly because users may be delayed until the writes occur.

Also, a before image of a page is put in the physical log buffer the first time it is updated between checkpoints. The physical log buffer is flushed to disk:

- When it is full.

- Whenever page cleaners flush any changed pages to disk. It is imperative that the before-image of a page be put on disk before its corresponding changed page is written.

The Root Dbspace

It is a good practice not to place any databases or tables in the root dbspace. The root dbspace contains some essential control information about the OnLine system. In INFORMIX-OnLine, the root dbspace will also be used for temporary tables (created with SELECT INTO TEMP). With INFORMIX-OnLine Dynamic Server, temporary tables can be redirected to another dbspace.

The Tables

The goal in placement of database tables is to spread the I/O workload across disks and controllers. You specify the dbspace in which the table will be placed using the CREATE TABLE statement. Once you define the location with CREATE TABLE, you cannot change the location except by dropping the table and re-creating it. That is why it is important to spend some time analyzing the optimal location of tables on disk.

Before deciding where tables should be placed, perform an analysis of the applications that access the tables. How often are each of the tables accessed during peak periods? What tables are accessed together? From this information, you can now begin to diagram a possible strategy for table placement.

You can perform your own striping by storing a table across several disks. Large tables will be spread across disks anyway because the data won't fit on one disk. To stripe a table, create a dbspace and add chunks on each disk. The example in Figure 4.6 shows a dbspace (**dbspace1**) with three chunks, with each chunk on a separate disk. The table **t1** is created in **dbspace1**. When rows are added to table **t1**, they will be added to the extent that will be created in the first free chunk, **chunk1**. When the first extent is filled, OnLine will create a new extent on the first free chunk; if the first chunk does not have enough free space to hold the extent, it will be created on the second chunk. You do not have any direct control over which chunk the rows are created in.

Figure 4.6-Striping a table across disks

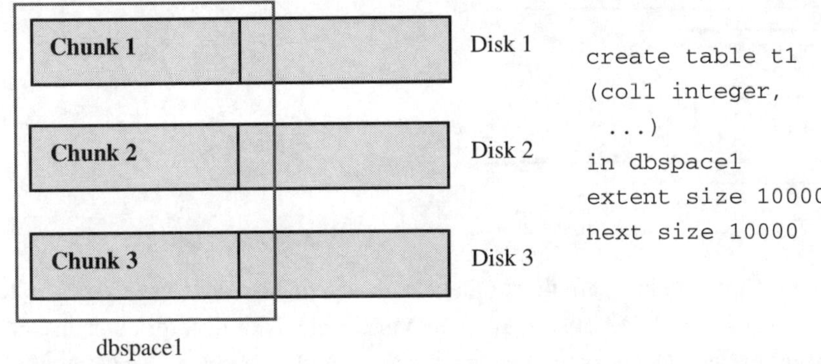


```
create table t1
(col1 integer,
   ...)
in dbspace1
extent size 10000
next size 10000
```

From this discussion it follows that if **t1** starts out small, the rows will be located on only one disk. You will not receive any striping benefits until the table grows. However, you can "trick" the OnLine system into placing the second and third extents in disk 2 and 3 by creating dummy tables with large extent sizes in **dbspace1**. Say, for example, that each chunk is 25 Mbytes. Table **t1** is created with the first extent of 10 Mbytes. If you create a dummy table with an extent of 10 Mbytes, this reserves 10 Mbytes of space that cannot be used for table **t1** (you do not have to add any rows to the dummy table). When table **t1** needs another extent, it will be created on the next free chunk, **chunk2**, because there are not 10 Mbytes of free space on **chunk1**! You can later drop the dummy table as t1 grows across three disks.

If you have many small to medium-sized tables that are heavily used, you may not want to stripe tables. For example, if 50 users are all executing a transaction that updates four tables on two disks, each table is being accessed approximately the same amount. By putting two tables on one disk and two tables on another disk, you are effectively spreading the work evenly across disks without striping. As shown in Figure 4.7, this disk layout would require only two dbspaces.

4.12 LIMIT ON THE NUMBER OF CHUNKS

The limitation on the maximum number of chunks in INFORMIX-OnLine may constrain the way you configure disks. The maximum number of chunks is the lower of these two values:

Figure 4.7-Table layout without striping

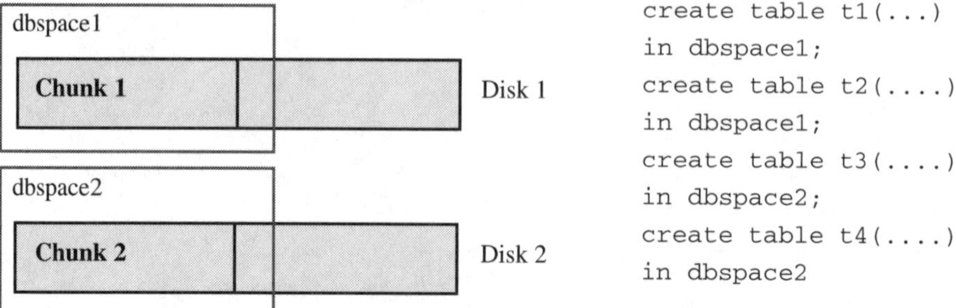


```
create table t1(...)
in dbspace1;
create table t2(....)
in dbspace1;
create table t3(....)
in dbspace2;
create table t4(....)
in dbspace2
```

- The number of chunk path names that can fit onto a page. One page keeps both the chunk name and the location (path name) of the chunk of disk for all chunks in the OnLine system. One way to allow more chunks in the OnLine system is to keep the chunk path names to a minimum. If you are using raw devices, you should use a symbolic link to the device name. Symbolic links can help shorten the device name as well as being a good idea in case the disk goes down and needs to be replaced (you can relink the symbolic name to another disk device). For example,

```
ln -s /dev/rsd01e /I/chk1
```

- The number of available file descriptors that can be used by a process. This is an operating system limit. On most versions of UNIX, you can increase the open files per process by adjusting a UNIX kernel parameter.

The first limitation may keep the number of chunk path names down to approximately 30–40 chunks. This might not seem like a limitation, but this means that with ten disks used for OnLine, only three or four chunks can be created on each disk. This severely limits the amount of disk striping you can implement at the OnLine system level for large databases.

In INFORMIX-OnLine Dynamic Server the limit on the maximum number of chunks is 2048.

4.13 EASE OF ADMINISTRATION

With more dbspaces and chunks in an OnLine system, the administrator has to pay closer attention to the free space in each dbspace. Remember that an ALTER TABLE statement often must create a complete copy of the table being altered in the same dbspace as the one in which the table resides. With one table per dbspace, you don't have a pool of free space in which to perform an ALTER TABLE. Also, with more dbspaces, you must monitor each to make sure there is enough free space allocated to handle the growth in a table. If one table grows more than you expected, you may have to rearrange dbspaces to obtain more space for the larger table.

Rearranging usage of dbspaces is difficult. To reassign disk space from one dbspace to another, you must drop a chunk (only allowed in INFORMIX-OnLine Dynamic Server) or dbspace and readd that space to another dbspace. However, the chunks that are being dropped must be completely empty, meaning you must first drop the tables that have extents in that chunk before dropping the chunk. A better way to manage growth of tables is to leave some empty disk space unassigned to dbspaces. If more space is needed, you can simply add a new chunk using the previously unassigned disk space.

4.14 TEMPORARY TABLES AND FILES

A decision support query (a query that reads and manipulates a large amount of data) can use a large amount of temporary disk space. The disk space can be used for sorting, hash tables (for joins), and temporary tables that are created with the INTO TEMP clause or explicitly by the application. Systems that emphasize decision support queries should also make temporary table and file space a priority.

INFORMIX-OnLine stores temporary tables in the root dbspace or the dbspace you specify in the CREATE TEMP TABLE statement. Temporary files are stored in file system space (**/tmp** by default or the directory specified by PSORT_DBTEMP). You can specify multiple disks only with the PSORT_DBTEMP environment variable, and a sort using temporary file space will be spread across multiple disks. You must also set PSORT_NPROCS to the number of processes that will be started to perform the sort. For example,

```
PSORT_NPROCS=3
PSORT_DBTEMP=/tempdb1,/tempdb2,/tempdb3
```

INFORMIX-OnLine Dynamic Server stores temporary files and tables (created by the INTO TEMP clause) in the dbspace or dbspaces specified by the DBSPACETEMP configuration parameter and environment variable. You can spread temporary files across disks by specifying multiple dbspaces in the DBSPACETEMP configuration parameter (or by the environment variable which overrides the configuration parameter):

```
DBSPACETEMP dbs1,dbs2,dbs3
```

Each of the dbspaces should have chunks on separate disks.

4.15 DISK PLACEMENT PRIORITIES

As a review, here are the priorities in disk placement of the various components of an OnLine system. For decision support systems (emphasis placed on queries that read a large amount of data) or databases without logging, the priorities are as follows:

- Most used tables,
- Temporary sort and table space,
- Least used tables, and
- Logical and physical logs.

For transaction-oriented systems, the priorities are as follows:

- Logical and physical logs,
- Most used tables,
- Least used tables, and
- Temporary sort and table space.

With one disk, there are not many choices in the placement of the OnLine structures. Figure 4.8 shows four dbspaces, one for the root dbspace, one for the logical and physical logs, one for the data and one for the temporary files and tables.

Figure 4.8-Sample disk layout with one disk

root dbspace	logs dbspace	tables dbspace	temporary tables dbspace

For two disks and an OnLine system that has OLTP activity, you can put the root dbspace and the logical and physical logs on one disk and the data on another (see Fig. 4.9). Another strategy, which would be preferable for decision support systems, is to put some tables on disk 1 and some tables on disk 2.

For three or more disks, you have more choices (see Fig. 4.10). For high OLTP systems with a large database, it would benefit you to place the logical logs on their own disk. The reasoning behind this philosophy is that the writes to the logical log are sequential. The disk head would be placed in the correct position at all times to write to the logical log if there is nothing else placed on that disk. If the logical logs don't take up the full disk, consider putting infrequently used tables in a dbspace on the same disk. For decision support systems, you would spread tables across all three disks and create two dbspaces for temporary tables and files (each on separate disks).

Figure 4.9-Sample disk layout with two disks

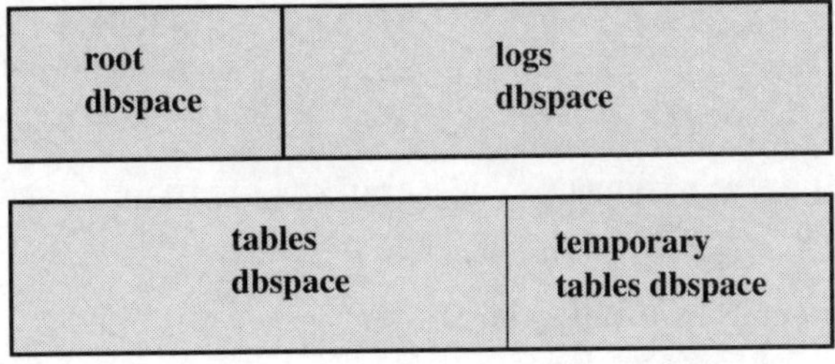

Figure 4.10-Sample disk layout with three or more disks

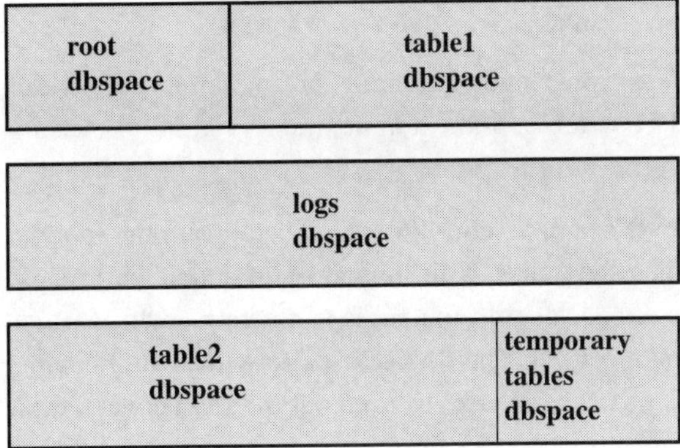

4.16 MONITORING DISK LAYOUT

After you get data loaded into your proposed disk layout, you can check the results of your work in INFORMIX-OnLine by running **tbstat -D**. In INFORMIX-OnLine Dynamic Server, you can run **onstat -g iof**. With the output from this command you can see the I/O that occurred on each chunk since the last time the OnLine system was brought down, or since the last **onstat -z** cleared the statistics.

A sample output from **tbstat -D** follows:

```
Dbspaces
address    number flags fchunk nchunks flags owner      name
818480     1      1     1      1        N    informix   rootdbs
818480     2      1     2      1        N    informix   dbs2

2 active, 8 total
```

```
Chunks
address    chk/dbs    offset    page Rd    page Wr    pathname
817e94     1    1      0         31082      199065     /dev/chunk6
817f2c     2    2      0         2520       3807       /dev/chunk7
2 active,  8 total
```

The **page Rd** and **page Wr** columns show the amount of disk reads and writes for all the tables in each chunk.

A sample output from **onstat -g iof** follows:

```
AIO global files
gfd     pathname      totalops    dskread    dskwrite    io/s
3       /dev/chunk1    2520        2350        170        0.1
4       /dev/chunk2    950         614         336        0.0
5       /dev/chunk3    17887       5852        12035      0.4
```

In either output, you cannot determine the amount of I/O for each table, unless the dbspace holds only one table. Some administrators put highly used tables in their own dbspaces just to get this information.

In the **tbstat -D** example, **chunk6**, which belongs to the root dbspace, is receiving most of the disk reads and writes. In the **onstat -g iof** output, **chunk3** is receiving the most I/O. Your next step after seeing this output is to determine what OnLine objects are in the chunk receiving the most I/O. The **tbcheck -pe (oncheck -pe)** command can be used to see the exact contents of the chunk. To even out the I/O between these two chunks, you could move some objects in the root dbspace to dbs2.

You should also monitor disk I/O at the UNIX level with the **sar** or **iostat** utility to get an idea of the disk utilization levels.

4.17 SPECIAL CONSIDERATIONS FOR THE INFORMIX-ONLINE DYNAMIC SERVER

INFORMIX-OnLine Dynamic Server I/O is controlled by a set of I/O vps. The LIO vp handles logical-log I/O. The PIO vp handles physical-log I/O. The AIO vps handle all other I/O, both reads and writes, on behalf of the sessions and the page cleaners. The page cleaner processes in INFORMIX-OnLine become threads running on the CPU vps in INFORMIX-OnLine Dynamic Server.

On some operating systems, the actual disk I/O is handled not by the AIO vps but by the UNIX kernel. This type of I/O is known as *kernel AIO* and can add a significant performance boost to I/O processing. However, it is used for OnLine I/O only on certain systems. Check the machine notes file in the **$INFORMIXDIR/release** directory to determine whether kernel AIO is being used or not. Even if the product supports it, kernel

AIO will be used only on chunks that were created using raw devices. Chunks created on file system files (or cooked chunks) will continue to use the AIO vps.

The AIO vps monitor their queue for requests and service each request, performing the I/O by reading dirty pages from the buffer pool and writing them to disk.

The INFORMIX-OnLine Dynamic Server release offers an additional set of parameters that should be tuned. They are

- Number of AIO vps and
- Read-aheads.

Number of AIO vps

If your OnLine system is using kernel AIO for all I/O, configuring the number of AIO vps is easy. The AIO vps will be used only for I/O to files such as the $ONCONFIG file or the message log. You need configure only one or two AIO vps—one for a smaller system, two for a larger system.

If you have chunks residing on file system files (not raw devices) or your OnLine system does not use kernel AIO, configuring the number of AIO vps becomes very important. You do not want AIO vps to have a long backlog of requests for I/O. You can monitor the backlog of AIO requests by running **onstat -g ioq**. This command shows the current length of the I/O queue (**len**) for each of the AIO vps and the largest the AIO queue has ever been (**maxlen**). Since each AIO vp has its own queue, the report will show one line for every AIO vp. A sample output of **onstat -g ioq**, showing two AIO queues, follows:

```
class/hvp-id len   maxlen   totalops   dskread   dskwrite   dskcopy
adt     0     0     0        0          0         0          0
msc     0     0     1        3          0         0          0
aio     0     0     150      26725      18589     8136       0
aio     1     0     150      1254       940       314        0
pio     0     0     0        0          0         0          0
lio     0     0     0        0          0         0          0
```

A clever indication that the OnLine system is using kernel AIO is the appearance of a kio queue in this output. If you see the kio queue and you are using raw devices, set the number of AIO vps to 1.

To monitor the AIO queues, bring up the OnLine system and then run **onstat -z** to clear out statistics (the queue length becomes abnormally high when the OnLine system first comes up), and then monitor the **len** and **maxlen** columns over a period of time. If the current queue lengths are often greater than 0, you can try adding an AIO vp.

You can configure the number of AIO vps by the NUMAIOVPS configuration parameter or by dynamically adding AIO vps while the OnLine system is up using **onmonitor**.

Read-Aheads

The optimal behavior of the OnLine system is for a session reading data to never have to wait for a disk read. The best way to cut down on disk reads is to somehow second-guess the next page that the user will need and read it from disk into the buffer pool before the page is requested by a user. This mechanism is called *read-ahead*. OnLine will perform a read-ahead under several circumstances:

1. The optimizer determines that a SELECT will perform a sequential scan. An example of a SELECT that will probably perform a sequential read is

   ```
   SELECT *    from tab1
   ```

2. The optimizer determines that a SELECT will read the index sequentially and that all the needed columns are part of the index. Another term for this case is a key-only search. An example of a SELECT that will probably perform a key-only search (assuming **col1** has an index) is

   ```
   SELECT col1 from table1 where col1 > 200
   ```

3. The optimizer senses that a SELECT will read the index sequentially but must retrieve the data page as well. An example of this kind of SELECT (assuming **col1** has an index) is

   ```
   SELECT * from table 1 where col1 > 20
   ```

You can alter read-ahead configuration parameters that affect sequential scans (number 1 above). These parameters are

- **RA_PAGES.** The number of pages that are read ahead.
- **RA_THRESHOLD.** The number of pages of the RA_PAGES group that are left to be read by the session before another RA_PAGES is read.

For example, if RA_PAGES is set to four and RA_THRESHOLD is set to one, four pages would be read ahead and put in the buffer pool. After the third page is read by the session (one page left to be read), four more pages would be read ahead and put in the buffer pool. This ensures that the read-ahead mechanism is always slightly ahead of the session.

The number of pages read ahead by index scans cannot be directly modified by read-ahead parameters. Instead, they are a function of the number of active sessions and the buffer pool size.

Usually, the default read-ahead parameters should be sufficient. However, if you are doing a great deal of sequential reading (for example, with index builds), you may want to increase the read-ahead values somewhat. If you set the read-ahead parameters too high, the extra pages put in the buffer pool may replace pages of data needed by other sessions, requiring them to perform a disk read instead. You can see evidence of read-aheads set too high if the read cache rate decreases.

In addition to the cache rate, **onstat -p** also shows how many pages are being read ahead.

```
ixda-RA    idx-RA    da-RA    RA-pgsused
2          0         3182     3093
```

The **ixda-RA** column is the number of data pages read ahead because of a sequential read of an index. The **idx-RA** column shows the number of index pages read ahead because of a key-only read operation. The **da-RA** column is the number of pages read ahead in a sequential scan. And **RA-pgsused** is the number of read-ahead pages actually used by the session.

Unfortunately, there is no good way to tell whether you have set the read-ahead parameters sufficiently, other than timing performance of certain activities that read pages sequentially.

4.18 CASE STUDY

The users start to complain about intermittently slow response times during busy times of the day. After monitoring system CPU usage to make sure the system is not overloaded, you decide to check the OnLine system.

The slow response time might be occurring during a checkpoint. Because a checkpoint can stop all critical actions (writing to a page, for example), users might be waiting for a long checkpoint to complete.

You run **onstat -RF** to determine how many disk writes are occurring during the checkpoint:

```
Fg Writes    LRU Writes   Chunk Writes
0            24879        3773
```

In this example, the bulk of the writes are occurring between checkpoints. However, there is a significant number of chunk writes (writes occurring during a checkpoint), so it might be worthwhile to tune the LRU parameters (LRU_MAX_DIRTY and LRU_MIN_DIRTY) to decrease this number.

Also, the checkpoint duration once during the testing cycle was fairly long (25 seconds), as shown in **onstat -m** (note that this is an option in INFORMIX-OnLine Dynamic Server; you must physically time the checkpoint duration if using INFORMIX-OnLine):

```
16:03:40 Checkpoint Completed: duration was 13 seconds
16:08:28 Checkpoint Completed: duration was 25 seconds
16:13:49 Checkpoint Completed: duration was 7 seconds
16:19:05 Checkpoint Completed: duration was 10 seconds
```

One possible symptom users may see during long checkpoint durations is that transactions seem to "hang" momentarily, waiting for the checkpoint to complete.

To decrease the chunk writes (writes that occur during checkpoints) and hopefully decrease the checkpoint duration, you decide to decrease LRU_MAX_DIRTY and LRU_MIN_DIRTY. By increasing LRU_MAX_DIRTY to 10 and LRU_MIN_DIRTY to 5, most of the disk writes occur between checkpoints.

The **onstat -RF** output after this change looks like

```
Fg Writes     LRU Writes    Chunk Writes
0             32551         2632
```

You rerun **onstat -m** and find that the checkpoint duration decreases:

```
17:03:30 Checkpoint Completed: duration was 1 seconds
17:08:18 Checkpoint Completed: duration was 7 seconds
17:13:39 Checkpoint Completed: duration was 7 seconds
17:18:56 Checkpoint Completed: duration was 7 seconds
```

Table 4.1 summarizes the important aspects of disk tuning.

Table 4.1–Disk-tuning checklist

What to Check	How to Check	How to Alter
Read cache rate	onstat -p	BUFFERS configuration parameter
Write cache rate	onstat -p	BUFFERS configuration parameter
Checkpoint interval	onstat -m	CKPTINTVL configuration parameter or physical log size
Checkpoint duration	onstat -m (or by manual timing in INFORMIX-OnLine)	LRU_MAX_DIRTY, LRU_MIN_DIRTY, CKPTINTVL configuration parameters or physical log size
Page cleaning	onstat -RF	CLEANERS, LRU_MAX_DIRTY, LRU_MIN_DIRTY, LRUs, BUFFERS configuration parameters
Disk placement	tbstat -D or onstat -g iof, iostat, sar	Change arrangement of items on disk
Read ahead (INFORMIX-Online Dynamic Server)	onstat -p	RA_PAGES, RA_THRESHOLD
AIO vps (INFORMIX-OnLine Dynamic Server)	onstat -g ioq	NUMAIOVPS

Chapter 5

Memory Performance

This chapter discusses how memory can affect performance of the OnLine system. Memory is a performance factor only if there is not enough of it to do the required work. The major topics discussed in this chapter follow:

- The types of memory to monitor
- Computing memory requirements
- How to monitor memory
- Tips for decreasing the use of memory
- How to calculate the amount of memory needed

5.1 THE TYPES OF MEMORY TO MONITOR

Memory takes one of two forms in an OnLine system: process memory and shared memory. *Process memory* refers to the memory needed for database server processes. *Shared memory* holds information used by all database server processes, such as the buffer cache, the lock and latch structures, and the logical log buffer.

INFORMIX-OnLine Memory

One INFORMIX-OnLine database server process (**sqlturbo**) runs for each user. The data portion of memory for each process is dynamic and grows independently as needed for each user (see Fig. 5.1). For example, if the user executes a large stored procedure, the code for the stored procedure is brought in to the database server process and put in a cache of stored procedures specifically for reuse by the same user. To determine how much memory the database server processes are using, you should monitor each process during a period of average activity.

Figure 5.1-INFORMIX-OnLine memory

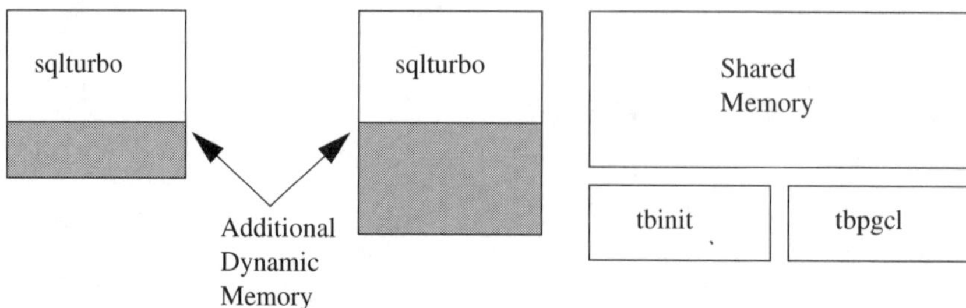

In addition to the database server processes, there is a master process, called **tbinit**, that coordinates activities such as the initialization of shared memory and checkpoints. The size of this process generally remains the same.

There is also a set of page cleaner processes that handle writing pages from memory to disk. These processes are listed by **ps** as **tbpgcl**, or sometimes as **tbinit**, because they are started as child processes to the master **tbinit** process.

Finally, you may see sort processes if you are running parallel sorts.

The amount of shared memory used for OnLine remains static while the OnLine system is up. The size of OnLine shared memory is altered by changing the shared memory configuration parameters. The main determinant of the total size of shared memory is the size of the buffer cache.

INFORMIX-OnLine Dynamic Server Memory

In INFORMIX-OnLine Dynamic Server, the work of all users is accomplished by a few (approximately 7–20) database server processes since the processes are multithreaded. The database server processes, or virtual processors, start when OnLine comes up and stay running until OnLine stops. The **ps** listing shows the virtual processors running as **oninit**. The process sizes of the vps remain the same while they are running.

The shared memory requirements for the INFORMIX-OnLine Dynamic Server increase dramatically from INFORMIX-OnLine, mainly because shared memory holds much of the data previously held in the **sqlturbo** processes (see Fig. 5.2). The OnLine shared memory is divided into three parts:

- **Resident.** This shared memory is very similar to the shared memory in INFORMIX-OnLine. It is static and contains structures such as the buffer cache, locks, and logical and physical logs.

- **Virtual.** This shared memory contains structures needed mainly by the multi-threaded subsystem, such as each user thread's stack. Virtual memory is organized in *pools*, where each pool is used for a specific purpose. Each pool is allocated as needed and released when no longer needed. Because the multithreaded database server allows a thread to run on multiple processes, the pools must be localized in shared memory so they can be accessed by all virtual processors. The virtual shared memory may grow as needed as users connect and execute SQL statements.

- **Message.** This shared memory is used as a bulletin board for messages between the client and database server processes. This shared memory is static and is configurable by setting the maximum number of shared memory connections in the OnLine configuration file.

Figure 5.2-INFORMIX-OnLine Dynamic Server memory

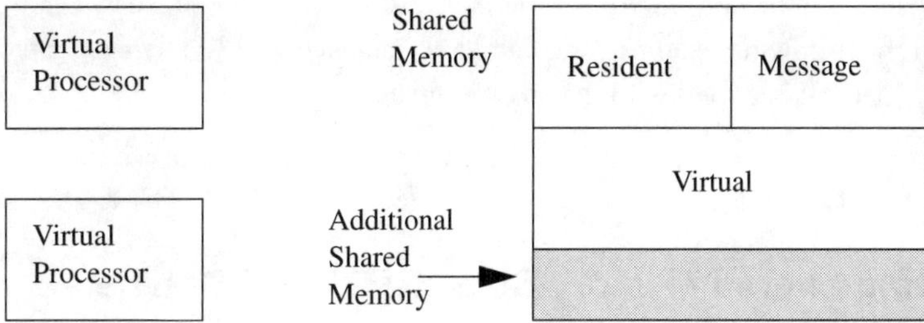

Application Memory

Although application processes are not discussed in detail in this book, it is worth mentioning that you should take application process memory into account when calculating total memory requirements. If applications are running on the same machine as OnLine, they could potentially take up much of the total memory.

5.2   COMPUTING MEMORY REQUIREMENTS

Process Memory

Each process is made up of three parts: the text (or code size), the stack, and the data. INFORMIX database server processes share the same code, or text space, so this amount must be accounted for only once for all occurrences of the same process.

You can use the UNIX **size** command to determine the fixed size of a process (not including any extra memory added as the process is running). For example, to run the **size** command for the **sqlturbo** process (for INFORMIX-OnLine):

```
% size sqlturbo
text           data         bss         dec          hex
1171456     122880       12640       1306976       13f160
```

In this example, the text size is 1,171,456 bytes or 1.12 Mbytes. The data and stack can be calculated by adding the **data** and **bss** columns. The example shows the data and stack to be 122,880 + 12,640 = 148,160 bytes or approximately 144 kbytes.

Since the **sqlturbo** process (INFORMIX-OnLine) grows during its execution, you must monitor the process size during levels of average and peak activity to determine the maximum amount of memory it needs. You can use the UNIX **ps** command to determine the size of the data and stack at any one point in time. Using BSD UNIX, run the following command:

```
ps -aux|grep sqlturbo
```

To determine the current size of the data and stack for the process, examine the SZ column. In the following example, the data and stack size is 180 kbytes, about 46 kbytes more than what was reported with the **size** command.

```
USER    PID   %CPU   %MEM   SZ   RSS   TT   STAT   START TIME   COMMAND
joe     3097  0.0    0.0    180  0     p3   IW     12:48 0:00   sqlturbo
```

Estimating Shared Memory Size: INFORMIX-OnLine

Estimating the size of INFORMIX-OnLine shared memory is easy. The **tbmonitor** tool automatically calculates the approximate size based on the configuration parameters you enter. Choose the **Parameters:Shared Memory** option to get the screen that looks like Figure 5.3.

Figure 5.3-Parameters: Shared memory option

```
                        SHARED MEMORY PARAMETERS

Page Size                               [     2] Kbytes

Server Number                           [    0]        Server Name [ONLINE          ]
Deadlock Timeout                        [   60] Seconds
Forced Residency                        [N]
Number of Page Cleaners          [    1]

Physical Log Buffer Size  [          32] Kbytes
Logical Log Buffer Size   [          32] Kbytes
Max # of Logical Logs          [     6]
Max # of Users            [         20]
Max # of Locks            [       2000]
Max # of Buffers          [        200]
Max # of Chunks                [     8]
Max # of Open Tblspaces        [   200]
Max # of Dbspaces              [     8]
                          =============
Shared memory size              [    768] Kbytes
```

As you adjust the parameters in brackets that affect the shared memory size, the **Shared memory size** field at the bottom of the screen is recalculated. The configuration parameters that affect the shared memory size are the physical and logical log buffers, the maximum number of users, the maximum number of locks, the maximum number of buffers, the maximum number of chunks, the maximum number of open tablespaces, and the maximum number of dbspaces. The parameter that changes shared memory most significantly is the maximum number of buffers.

You can also see the size of shared memory once OnLine is running with any **tbstat** command. The top part of the output reports the shared memory size in kbytes. The following example shows an OnLine system that is using approximately 10.3 Mbytes.

```
RSAM Version 5.00.UC1D3--On-Line--Up 00:13:10--10552 Kbytes
```

Estimating Shared Memory Size: INFORMIX-OnLine Dynamic Server

The INFORMIX-OnLine Dynamic Server resident shared memory segments can be calculated using **onmonitor** through the **Parameters:Shared Memory** menu option. The screen looks like that in Figure 5.4.

Figure 5.4-Calculation of shared memory segments with onmonitor

```
                         SHARED MEMORY PARAMETERS
Server Number                      [   6]            Server Name [onlineshm          ]
Server Aliases  [                                                                    ]
Dbspace Temp    [                                                                    ]
Deadlock Timeout                   [  60] Secs  Number of Page Cleaners    [    1]
Forced Residency                      [N]       Stack Size (Kbytes)        [   32]
Non Res. SegSize (Kbytes)     [   8000]

Physical Log Buffer Size  [           32] Kbytes
Logical Log Buffer Size   [           32] Kbytes
Max # of Logical Logs           [    6]            Transaction Timeout     [ 300]
Max # of Transactions     [          60]           Long TX HWM             [  70]
Max # of Userthreads      [          60]           Long TX HWM Exclusive   [  80]
Max # of Locks            [        2000]           Index Page Fill Factor  [  90]
Max # of Buffers          [         400]
Max # of Chunks                 [    8]
Max # of Open Tblspaces         [  200]
Max # of Dbspaces               [    8]
                          ============
Shared memory size        [        1264] Kbytes           Page Size [     2] Kbytes
```

As you adjust the configuration parameters that affect the resident size, you will see the **Shared memory size** field at the bottom of the screen increase. The configuration parameters that affect the resident size are the physical and logical log buffers, the maximum number of user threads, the maximum number of locks, the maximum number of buffers, the maximum number of chunks, the maximum number of open tablespaces, and the maximum number of dbspaces. The parameter that changes the resident portion of shared memory most significantly is the maximum number of buffers. Note that starting with version 7.10.UD1, certain configuration parameters are eliminated (USER-THREADS, TRANSACTIONS, CHUNKS, TBLSPACES, DBSPACES) because the structures in the resident portion are allocated automatically and will grow as needed.

The message shared memory segments tend to be relatively small and are calculated from the number of shared memory connections specified in the NETTYPE parameter. The NETTYPE parameter has several fields—the third field specifies the number of connections. In the following example, 50 connections are allowed via shared memory:

```
NETTYPE ipcshm,1,50,CPU
```

The formula for calculating the approximate message segment size in bytes is as follows:

```
(10,531 * #connections) + 50,000
```

Using the NETTYPE parameter shown previously with 50 connections, the size of the message segment would be (10,531 * 50) + 50,000, or approximately 563 kbytes.

The size of virtual shared memory segments you need is very difficult to estimate. This is because memory is allocated as needed by individual sessions. If the virtual segments cannot handle the memory needed by a session, another shared memory segment is automatically allocated by OnLine. Shared memory segments are not deallocated until the OnLine system is brought down.

As a rule of thumb, each session running basic SQL statements will need around 100 kbytes of virtual shared memory. However, the following things can really increase the amount of shared memory needed by a session:

- Sorts,
- Hash tables (for hash joins),
- Large stored procedures, and
- **oncheck** runs.

For example, a sort can be anywhere from 100 kbytes to 1.5 Mbytes, depending on the size of the columns being sorted. If your applications have any SELECT statements with an ORDER BY clause or if you are creating indexes, you should estimate approximately 500 kbytes per session during peak periods.

OnLine will use as much memory as it can (based on internal algorithms) for hash tables and sort space. If more space is needed, temporary disk space will be used.

5.3 HOW TO MONITOR MEMORY

Shared Memory Usage

UNIX allocates memory in units of a segment. How many segments OnLine uses depends upon several things: the UNIX kernel segment size, the amount of memory initially requested by OnLine, and the amount of memory required once the OnLine system is up (INFORMIX-OnLine Dynamic Server only).

The UNIX kernel segment size is specified by the SHMMAX or SHMSIZE kernel parameter (the parameter name varies from system to system). Suppose the SHMMAX parameter is set at 1 Mbyte and OnLine requests 10 Mbytes of shared memory. In this case, ten UNIX shared memory segments are created.

You will want to monitor the number of shared memory segments created as well as the amount of shared memory used. Some operating systems have a limit to the number of segments that can be created. Most operating systems constrain the number of segments by a kernel parameter (SHMMNI).

The UNIX **ipcs** command lists each shared memory segment and its appropriate size.

```
%ipcs -m

IPC status from prod as of Sun Jan 23 13:32:17 1994
T ID KEY            MODE        OWNER     GROUP      SEGSZ
Shared Memory:
m 0 0x52574801 --rw-rw---- informix informix   1048576
m 1 0x52574802 --rw-rw---- informix informix   1048576
m 2 0x52574803 --rw-rw---- informix informix   1048576
m 3 0x52574804 --rw-rw---- informix informix   1048576
m 4 0x52574805 --rw-rw---- informix informix    819200
```

In the preceding example, five shared memory segments have been allocated with a total of (1,048,576 * 4 + 819,200) = 5,013,504 bytes or 4816 kbytes.

In INFORMIX-Online Dynamic Server, you can identify the type of each segment allocated with the **onstat -g seg** command. A sample output of this command follows:

```
Segment Summary:
  (resident segments are not locked)
id  key          addr     size     ovhd class blkused blkfree
100 1381779457 800000   2613248 780    R       315     4
103 1381779460 a7e000   8192000 696    V       288     712
11  1381779468 124e000 262144   576    M       29      3
```

In the preceding example, three segments are allocated, one for resident shared memory, one for virtual shared memory, and one for messages for shared memory communication. Each is identified as such in the **class** column. For each segment, you are shown the approximate amount of memory used and the amount of memory free in 8-kbyte blocks. This information is valuable only for the virtual segments. If the virtual segments show close to 0 blocks free, you know that another virtual segment will be allocated automatically as soon as a session requests more memory.

Determining If Memory Usage Is Too High

If there is an insufficient amount of memory in the operating system to handle the work load, UNIX will start *paging*; that is, pages in memory will be written to disk to make way for pages that are needed by running processes. Some paging is normal and acceptable, since there will be some pages in shared memory or in your program that are not needed most of the time. These pages can easily be moved to disk and probably will be, since UNIX uses a least recently used algorithm to decide which pages to move to disk. However, you will experience some performance degradation if UNIX starts to move pages that are needed often by the database server to disk.

In severely memory-starved systems, the operating system will begin to swap entire processes to disk. Any swapping occurring on most systems is very undesirable.

For BSD UNIX systems, the **vmstat** utility is helpful in determining if memory usage is too high. The **po** (page-out) column shows the amount of page-out activity in your system. In the following example, the system is in good shape, as **po** is close to or at 0.

```
procs  memory                page              disk          faults        cpu
 r b w avm fre    re at pi po fr de sr d0 d1 d2 d3 in   sy    cs   us sy id
 1 0 0 0    28688 0  6  0  1  2  0  0  0  4  2  5  46   254   116 5  2  93
 1 2 0 0    28636 0  0  0  0  0  0  0  0  31 18 31 282  1373  674 27 11 62
 1 3 0 0    28544 0  0  0  0  0  0  0  0  28 16 35 321  1386  699 29 13 58
```

For System V UNIX, the **sar -r** command shows how much free memory is available, and the **sar -p** command shows the number of page faults. If page faults are high, the system is short of memory.

```
sar -r 5 5
    09:18:21    freemem    freeswp
    09:18:26    9902       592384
    09:18:31    9941       592384
    09:18:36    9921       592384
    09:18:41    9922       592384
    09:18:46    9903       592384
    Average     9925       592384
```

```
sar -p 5 5
   09:20:27    vflt/s    pflt/s    pgfil/s    rclm/s
   09:20:32    9.94      0.00      0.00       0.00
   09:20:37    5.17      0.00      0.00 q     0.00
   09:20:42    4.56      0.00      0.00       0.00
   09:20:47    17.17     0.00      0.00       0.00
   09:20:52    4.17      0.00      0.00       0.00
   Average     8.19      0.00      0.00       0.00
```

5.4   SUGGESTIONS TO IMPROVE MEMORY USAGE

There is not much you can do to decrease the memory usage of the database server. It is probably more efficient and better off for overall performance to buy more memory. However, given that this might not be possible, there are some alternatives.

INFORMIX-OnLine

Some possible ways to limit memory usage for INFORMIX-OnLine systems follow.

- Decrease the size of the OnLine buffer cache. The biggest effect on shared memory usage is the number of buffers allocated with the BUFFERS configuration parameter. However, by decreasing the buffer cache, you may be impacting performance in another way, by increasing the amount of disk reads and writes.

- Limit the size of stored procedures. Sixteen of the most recently used stored procedures are cached in **sqlturbo** memory at all times. If stored procedures are large, this could mean that a great deal of memory could be allocated for the cache. By breaking a stored procedure into smaller stored procedures, you can decrease the total memory needed for stored procedures.

- Limit the size and number of sorts that you run. Although sorts use disks to hold intermediate sorted runs, the current working sort run is held in memory. The administrator does not have direct impact on the size of the sort run held in memory. However, as the size of the value being sorted increases, the size of the sort run increases as well. Unless necessary, you should avoid sorting large character strings. Sorts occur under the following circumstances:

  — SELECT statements using the ORDER BY clause or the GROUP BY clause where an index cannot be used. You can decrease sorting by adding an index on a column that is sorted frequently.

  — SELECT statements that the optimizer chooses to use a sort merge join to join two tables together. This most likely occurs when one or more of the join columns do not have indexes.

— Index builds. The key value is sorted before the index is built. You can bypass the sort routine by setting the NOSORTINDEX environment variable. However, index builds on larger tables will be *much slower* with NOSORTINDEX set.

INFORMIX-Online Dynamic Server

The INFORMIX-OnLine Dynamic Server allows you to place a cap on the amount of shared memory that is used by the OnLine system. The parameter SHMTOTAL is the total amount of shared memory that can be allocated for an OnLine system. If OnLine tries to allocate another shared memory segment because a session needs more memory and the SHMTOTAL limit is reached, the task for which the session needed memory will fail.

In addition to capping the shared memory used, you can also control how much shared memory is allocated when more memory is required. The SHMVIRTSIZE parameter is the amount of virtual shared memory allocated to the OnLine system when it is brought up. The default value for this parameter is 8000 kbytes and will most certainly need to be increased. The SHMADD parameter controls the amount of shared memory that is added when the system is up and more virtual shared memory is required. The default value is 8000 kbytes, which means that any time a session needs memory and can't get it from the existing virtual segments, another 8000 kbytes will be added. Figure 5.5 illustrates how these configuration parameters affect shared memory.

Figure 5.5-How configuration parameters affect shared memory

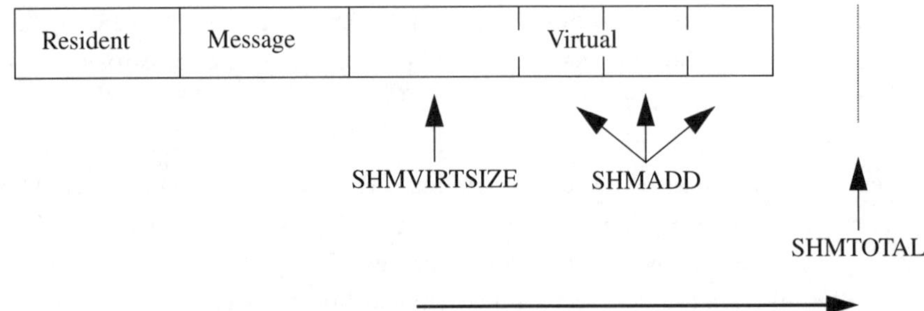

Once these segments have been allocated, they cannot be deallocated except by bringing down the OnLine system. Note, however, that shared memory pages are treated like any other memory. They can be paged out if real memory is needed for any other purpose. This can hurt performance, though, if the pages being written to swap area are needed by other running processes.

Other than capping the amount of shared memory allocated, here are some suggestions for reducing the amount of memory used by OnLine.

- Since the biggest users of memory for individual sessions are sorts, you may be able to decrease memory usage by limiting the number of sorts executed simultaneously by sessions.

- The biggest user of the resident shared memory is the buffer cache. You can change the size of the buffer cache with the BUFFERS configuration parameter. However, by decreasing the buffer cache, you may be impacting performance in another way, by increasing the amount of disk reads and writes.

- Avoid using Parallel Data Query. PDQ (which will be discussed in chapter 10) uses some memory for temporary space. You disable Parallel Data Query by setting PDQPRIORITY to 0. However, although you may be saving memory, you may also be losing overall performance by not parallelizing decision support queries.

- Avoid hash joins. The optimizer may choose a hash join if no index is on a join filter or if a large amount of data must be read from the table. You can avoid an automatic use of a hash join by adding an index on the join filter. Remember, however, that extra indexes require extra processing overhead for INSERT, UPDATE, and DELETE statements.

5.5 MEMORY CALCULATIONS

Tables 5.1 and 5.2 can be used to calculate the memory you will need for your OnLine database server. Some of the values in these worksheets should be obtained by monitoring a running OnLine system.

Table 5.1–Memory calculation worksheet (INFORMIX-OnLine)

	Text (shared)	Data (stack/data) (per process)	Shared Memory
sqlturbo processes			
tbinit processes			
Shared memory			
Total memory			

Table 5.2–Memory calculation worksheet (INFORMIX-OnLine Dynamic Server)

	Text (shared)	Data (stack/data) (per process)	Shared Memory
oninit processes			
Shared memory			
Total memory			

5.6   CASE STUDY—DETERMINING MEMORY USAGE FOR AN INFORMIX-ONLINE DYNAMIC SERVER SYSTEM

You manage an OnLine system that will be growing by 50 users in the next 6 months. You need to inform your management now if more memory is required for the added users.

You start by examining the current usage of the OnLine system. The **onstat -g seg** command shows the following shared memory, which has been allocated and represents the maximum amount required since the OnLine system was started:

```
onstat -g seg
```

id	key	addr	size	ovhd	class	blkused	blkfree
769	1381451777	800000	42000384	1432	R	5123	4
770	1381451778	300e000	61440000	1520	V	7442	58
771	1381451779	6aa6000	311296	588	M	35	3
516	1381451780	6af2000	16777216	836	V	1950	98
517	1381451781	7af2000	16777216	836	V	753	1295

From this output, you add up the entries in the size field to get 133,814 kbytes or 130 Mbytes. This number represents the amount of shared memory that has been allocated for the database server. Note that although 130 Mbytes has been allocated, the memory not currently used is paged out to disk.

To find out how much shared memory is actually allocated to session and overhead tasks, you add up the entries in the **blkused** column and multiply by 8 to get the approximate number of kilobytes currently used—122,424. This value is the representation of the total amount of shared memory needed on average by sessions that are currently running. You may run **onstat -g seg** and perform this calculation several times during the day to get a more representative sample of the amount of shared memory that is used at different times.

Next, you determine the size of the **oninit** processes from the **ps** command.

USER	PID	%CPU	%MEM	SZ	RSS	TT	STAT	START	TIME	COMMAND
root	22848	82.1	34.2	320	126948	p2	R	May 9	1385:24	oninit
root	22851	59.1	33.2	308	123112	p2	R	May 9	1009:57	oninit
root	22850	56.3	33.0	308	122704	p2	R	May 9	935:12	oninit
root	22849	0.0	0.3	296	1272	p2	S	May 9	3:43	oninit
root	22853	0.0	0.1	372	352	p2	S	May 9	6:36	oninit
root	22855	0.0	0.4	308	1432	p2	S	May 9	2:50	oninit
root	22852	0.0	0.4	308	1444	p2	S	May 9	2:53	oninit
root	22854	0.0	0.6	320	2396	p2	S	May 9	3:06	oninit

The data and stack size of each **oninit** process is approximately 320 kbytes. For eight oninit processes, the data and stack size used is 320 * 8 = 2560 kbytes.

By running a **size** command on the **oninit** process, you measure the size of the text portion of the process.

```
%size $INFORMIXDIR/bin/oninit
text        data        bss         dec         hex
2482176     237568      27552       2747296     29eba0
```

The text size is 2,482,176 bytes or 2424 kbytes.

From these two reports, you can now fill out the current memory calculation worksheet in Table 5.3.

Table 5.3–Current memory calculation data worksheet

	Text (shared)	Data (stack/data) (per process)	Shared Memory
oninit processes	2424 kbytes	320 kbytes	
Shared memory			122,424 kbytes
Total memory	2424 kbytes	2560 kbytes	122,424 kbytes

The total amount of memory currently used is 2424 + 2560 + 122,424 = 127,408 kbytes or approximately 124 Mbytes of memory.

Now you must determine how much memory the average user is allocating. The **onstat -g ses** command lists every active session. For each session id, you can run the following command:

```
onstat -g ses session_id
```

The output of this command lists, among other things, the shared memory pools that are currently allocated for the session. The output for some sessions looks like:

```
Memory pools count 2

name          class   addr      totalsize   freesize   #allocfrag   #freefrag
2117          V       35fa010   262144      48908      295          53
2117_SORT_0 V         3694010   352256      42044      7            6
```

This session is currently running a sort, as you notice from the SORT pool that is allocated. The total amount of memory for pools this session currently has allocated is 262,144 + 352,256 = 614,400 bytes or 600 kbytes.

```
Memory pools count 1

name            class  addr      totalsize  freesize  #allocfrag  #freefrag
2981            V      5fa2010   32768      5280      78          10
```

This session is using only 32,768 bytes or 32 kbytes.

```
Memory pools count 2

name            class  addr      totalsize  freesize  #allocfrag  #freefrag
2810            V      574e010   253952     47044     296         53
2810_SORT_0 V          3f40010   303104     28748     7
```

This session has allocated 253,952 + 303,104 bytes or 544 kbytes.

After examining the output from other sessions at different times of the day, you conclude that 500 kbytes per user is not unreasonable during peak periods of the day. For 50 new sessions running similar applications as the currently running sessions, you will need 50 * 500 kbytes or approximately an additional 25 Mbytes of memory during peak periods.

Chapter 6

CPU Usage and Performance

This chapter discusses how CPU usage affects database server performance and how the database server can be tuned to take full advantage of multiprocessor systems. The major topics discussed in this chapter follow:

- INFORMIX and multiprocessor systems
- How to monitor CPU usage
- What to expect in performance improvements by adding more processors
- How to tune processor usage in INFORMIX-OnLine
- How to tune processor usage in INFORMIX-OnLine Dynamic Server

6.1   INFORMIX AND MULTIPROCESSOR SYSTEMS

INFORMIX-OnLine and INFORMIX-OnLine Dynamic Server can run on single-processor systems, or on a special class of multiprocessor systems called *symmetrical multiprocessing* (SMP) systems. In an SMP system, processors are executing independent code but must communicate with other processors from time to time. A high-speed bus is used to connect all processors to each other and to a common set of memory. The number of processors that can effectively be used in a system depends heavily on the amount of traffic between processors that the bus can handle.

Parallel processing means that a task is split into pieces and processed in parallel. INFORMIX accomplishes parallel processing in INFORMIX-OnLine Dynamic Server by spreading tasks across processes, which in turn may be run on different processors in an SMP system. OnLine will act as a "scheduler" to assign threads to virtual processors. However, it is the responsibility of the UNIX scheduler to assign the virtual processors (which are simply processes) to a hardware processor.

6.2   HOW TO MONITOR CPU USAGE

On BSD UNIX systems, you can monitor the overall usage of the CPU with the **vmstat** command. An example output looks something like this:

```
procs memory              page            disk          faults        cpu
r b w avm fre    re at pi po fr de sr d0 d1 d2 d3 in  sy   cs  us sy id
1 0 0 0   28688 0  6  0  1  2  0  0  0  4  2  5  46  254  116 5  2  93
1 2 0 0   28636 0  0  0  0  0  0  0  0  31 18 31 282 1373 674 27 11 62
1 3 0 0   28544 0  0  0  0  0  0  0  0  28 16 35 321 1386 699 29 13 58
```

The columns that report information about CPU activity are the last three columns:

- The **us** column shows the percentage of the time the CPU was executing processes in the user state.

- The **sy** column shows the percentage of time the CPU was executing processes in the system state (kernel activity and other system overhead).

- The **id** column shows the percentage of time the CPU was idle.

The system in the example is in good shape, with 62 and 58% of the CPU idle during the sample time.

Another important piece of information is the first column, which displays the run queue. The run queue statistic is a count of the number of processes that are ready to run but are waiting, usually for CPU availability.

You can see System V UNIX processor activity with **sar -u**.

```
00:00:00    %usr    %sys    %wio    %idle
01:00:01    20      9       2       69
02:00:01    22      8       3       67
03:00:01    25      9       2       64
```

If the **%wio** value is significant in this output, your system may actually be I/O-bound, even if the **%idle** is low. You should investigate your disk performance in this case.

The System V command to monitor the run queue is **sar -q**.

For multiprocessor systems, it is helpful to view the activity of individual processors. Most multiprocessor systems have utilities to do this. For example, the multiprocessor SUN Microsystems machines have the **mpstat** utility, which gives the CPU utilization by processor.

```
average        cpu0        cpu1        cpu2        cpu3
us ni sy id us ni sy id us ni sy id us ni sy id us ni sy id
38 0  14 48 37  0 14 48 37 0  14 48 37 0  14 48 38 0  14 48
```

```
69 0   11 20 83   0 11   6 77 0   11 12 53 0   10 37 64 0   12 24
64 0   20 16 57   0 19 24 75 0   19 6   64 0   15 21 60 0   26 14
```

6.3 WILL ADDING ANOTHER PROCESSOR HELP PERFORMANCE?

INFORMIX-OnLine

In INFORMIX-OnLine, most of the work for one user is done within one process, the **sqlturbo** process. Consider a program, running by itself on a system, which performs an UPDATE statement to update one million rows into a table, using the **sqlturbo** process to perform each of the inserts serially. Even though the **sqlturbo** process can migrate from one processor to another on a multiprocessor system, it is running on only one processor at a time. This means that the UPDATE statement for one user does not take advantage of multiple hardware processors. In fact, an UPDATE statement running by itself on a machine generally *will not run significantly faster* on a multiprocessor machine than it will on a single-processor machine. This is a common mistake in thinking for administrators planning to upgrade their machine to a multiprocessor variety. Generally, it is the speed of the individual processor that will determine the speed of any individual database activity.

Now consider an OnLine system with 100 active users, each with its own **sqlturbo** process. If a single CPU system is showing 100% usage with 100 users, and the system run queue is consistently high, moving to a multiprocessor architecture or a single-processor system with a faster CPU will probably show performance improvements. With a multiprocessor system, each CPU can run an **sqlturbo** process simultaneously. Figure 6.1 illustrates the relationship between hardware processors and database server processes in INFORMIX-OnLine.

Does this mean that, if one CPU is at 100% capacity, doubling the number of processors will double performance? At some point while adding additional processors, other

Figure 6.1-Processor to database server process relationship (INFORMIX-OnLine)

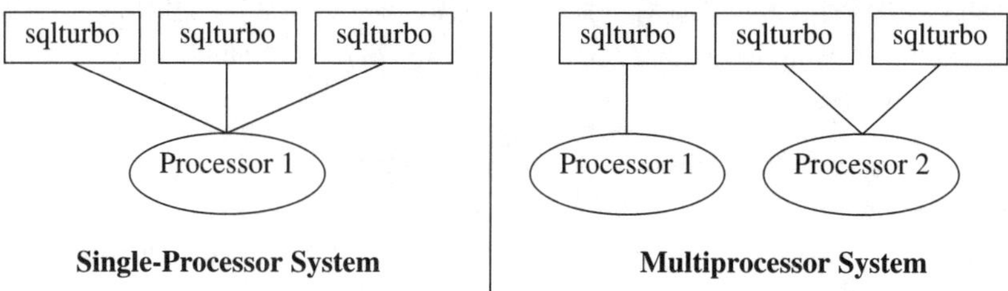

system bottlenecks (disk, memory, etc.) will prevent the system from using all of every processor for meaningful work.

INFORMIX-OnLine Dynamic Server

The INFORMIX-OnLine Dynamic Server is designed to work more efficiently with multiprocessor machines running many users. The CPU virtual processors do most of the CPU-intensive work for multiple users or sessions (see Fig. 6.2).

Figure 6.2-Processor to database server process relationship (INFORMIX-OnLine Dynamic Server)

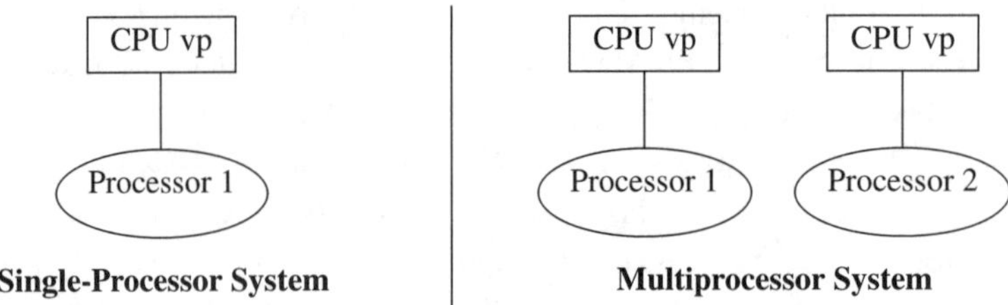

With the INFORMIX-OnLine Dynamic Server multithreaded architecture, each session can have multiple threads. Each thread can run on a separate CPU vp, effectively parallelizing an individual user's activity. In reality, the server only spawns multiple threads for the following activities:

- Queries,
- INSERTs (certain categories),
- Sorting,
- Index builds, and
- Database restores.

Parallel activities should run faster as you add more processors (and CPU vps). Each thread can run on different CPU vps, and each CPU vp can run on a different processor. This means that one session's query or CREATE INDEX statement can run on multiple processors at once (see Fig. 6.3).

For systems running INFORMIX-OnLine Dynamic Server, a processor overload may be evident only by the CPU idle time. The run queue in this case may be close to zero, because the CPU vps are the only processes within the OnLine system with heavy processor usage.

Figure 6.3-Parallelizing an activity (INFORMIX-OnLine Dynamic Server)

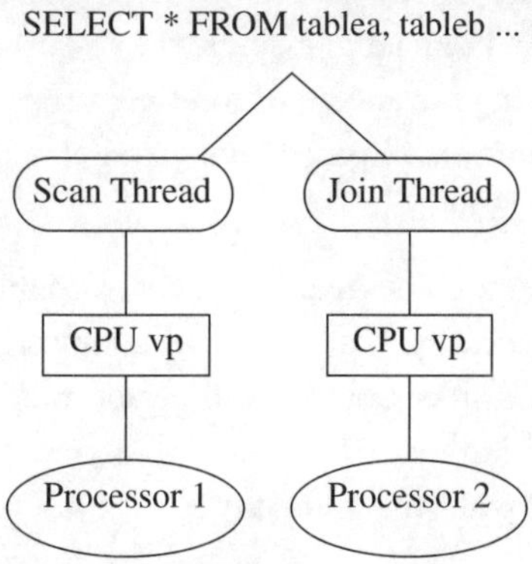

SELECT * FROM tablea, tableb ...

6.4 How to Influence Processor Usage in INFORMIX-OnLine

Beyond adding processors if you are CPU-bound, you can do a few things to affect the amount of processor usage:

- Move the application processes off the database server machine. Although there are inherent network delays added when you move the client applications to another machine, these network delays may be better than having an overloaded processor on the system running the database server.

- Modify the SPINCNT configuration parameter. When a database server process is waiting for another database server process to release a latch (an internal lock), it can do one of two things: sleep or keep trying to obtain the latch. Putting a process to sleep requires a small amount of overhead but is the appropriate thing to do on single-processor machines. However, with a multiprocessor system, it might make sense to avoid the expensive operation of putting the process to sleep and waking it up when the latch is available. When a database server process tries to obtain a latch, it runs in a loop, trying to obtain the latch every x iterations of the loop. As you can imagine, this can use up a significant amount of the processor if many database server processes are doing the same kind of waiting. You can determine the number of times the **sqlturbo** process tries for the latch by tuning the SPINCNT parameter. For example, by setting SPINCNT to 300, the database server tries to obtain the latch 300 times before giving up and going to sleep. If your CPU usage is high, you may want to decrease the SPINCNT parameter (the default is 300). By setting SPINCNT to zero, the process immediately goes to sleep on a latch wait. If you are using a single-processor machine, make sure SPINCNT is set to zero.

- Modify the use of parallel sorting. Multiprocessor systems usually benefit from using the parallel sorting feature. In INFORMIX-OnLine, this means that multiple sort processes are started to handle a single user's sort request. The sort processes can run in parallel, taking advantage of multiple processors. However, if the CPU idle time is relatively low on all processors, parallel sorting may slow down everything else running on a system.

To sort in parallel, you must set the environment variable PSORT_NPROCS before starting the client application process that will request the sort activity. PSORT_NPROCS should be set to the number of processes that will perform the sort. Generally, you should set PSORT_NPROCS to the number of processors in your system unless the hardware processors show a low %idle with **sar** or **vmstat**.

6.5 HOW TO INFLUENCE PROCESSOR USAGE IN INFORMIX-ONLINE DYNAMIC SERVER

Fortunately, you have more control over processor usage in the INFORMIX-OnLine Dynamic Server. Several tunable parameters affect how much processor is used for the database server.

The OnLine process that uses the most "user-state" processor time is the CPU vp. The AIO vp uses some processor time, but it is mostly "system-state" time.

The major tunable parameter that affects processor usage is the number of CPU virtual processors, set by the NUMCPUVPS configuration parameter. The CPU vp does most of the CPU-intensive work of the OnLine system. Generally, you should not have more than one CPU vp per processor. Having more than one per processor requires an increased number of operating system context switches, as the processor must service more processes. If other non-database processing occurs on the same machine, you may want to have significantly fewer CPU vps than hardware processors.

The best way to determine if you have enough CPU vps is to check the size of the OnLine ready queue. The OnLine ready queue (not to be confused with the system ready queue) is a list of all threads that are ready to run but lack a virtual processor to run on. Generally, you would like to see an empty or near-empty ready queue most of the time. You can see the number of ready threads by running **onstat -g rea**. A sample output looks like this:

```
Ready threads:
tid    tcb       rstcb   prty    status    vp-class    name
13     b53120       0    2       ready     1cpu        sm_discon
14     b5aed8   8067c4  2       ready     1cpu        flush_sub(0)
```

```
44      ca09a4   809dc4 2        ready    1cpu        sqlexec
45      ca946c   809a64 2        ready    1cpu        sqlexec
46      cb69a4   809704 2        ready    1cpu        sqlexec
```

In the preceding example, three user threads and two system threads are waiting for a free CPU vp to continue work.

If you are running on a single-processor machine, there is not much you can do about a ready queue that constantly has entries. On a multiprocessor machine, you can increase the number of CPU vps by one (until you reach the number of processors on your system) and continue monitoring the ready queue to see if the added processors helped. At some point, however, if CPU utilization for all processors is between 80 and 100%, adding another CPU vp can actually hurt performance.

To add a CPU vp dynamically, run the following command:

```
onmode -p +1 cpu
```

To drop a CPU vp dynamically, run the following command:

```
onmode -p -1 cpu
```

Adding or dropping a CPU vp dynamically does not change the number of CPU vps that will be started the next time the OnLine system comes up. Once you have determined an optimal number of CPU vps to start, modify the NUMCPUVPS configuration parameter or change the value in the **Parameters:perFormance** menu option of **onmonitor**.

Other Considerations

Other than altering the number of CPU vps, a few other considerations can improve performance in an INFORMIX-OnLine Dynamic Server system:

- Set the MULTIPROCESSOR configuration parameter to 1 for multiprocessor machines. This parameter primarily alters the OnLine system to use spin locks for threads. Thread spin locks keep threads from being put on a sleep or wait queue while waiting a very short time for a resource. Single-processor systems should set this parameter to 0.

- Set the SINGLE_CPU_VP parameter to 1 for single-processor systems. This constrains the OnLine system to use only one CPU vp and turns off some internal locking mechanisms because there is no contention for some resources by two CPU vps. The lack of these internal locks has such a positive effect on performance that even two processor systems may perform better with this parameter set to 1. However, this means that only one CPU vp can be started. For systems with more than two processors, set SINGLE_CPU_VP to 0.

- Modify use of Parallel Data Query. Multiprocessor systems usually benefit from using the PDQ feature. In INFORMIX-OnLine Dynamic Server, this means that multiple threads handle a single user's query. The threads can run in parallel, taking advantage of multiple processors. However, on a highly loaded system, parallel data query may slow down other operations, because the threads will be scheduled on the same CPU vps as the main session threads that perform other operations. If the OnLine ready queue is constantly loaded (**onstat -g rea**), turning off parallel operations may help performance. Parallel data query is turned on by a session if the PDQPRIORITY environment variable is set.

- Adjust processor affinity. Processor affinity allows a process to be bound to a single processor. By keeping a process on a processor, you take advantage of processor cache and forgo the overhead required to move a process from one hardware processor to another. Generally, you will want to set affinity on only CPU vps, since they perform the bulk of the work. OnLine has two configuration parameters that turn on processor affinity for systems that support it: AFF_NPROCS and AFF_SPROC. AFF_NPROCS specifies the number of hardware processors to which to assign CPU vps. For example, if AFF_NPROCS is 2, then two processors would run all CPU vps. Generally, you should set AFF_NPROCS to the number of CPU vps in the OnLine system and to a number less than the total number of hardware processors. The AFF_SPROC configuration parameter specifies the starting processor number for affinity (starting at 0). This allows you to pick certain processors to which to assign CPU vps (see Fig. 6.4).

Figure 6.4-Processor affinity example

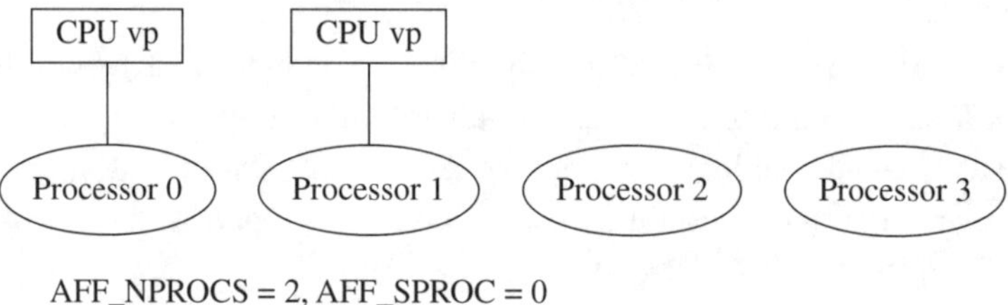

The number of hardware platforms that support the AFF_NPROCS and AFF_SPROC configuration parameters is limited (check your INFORMIX release notes). However, some operating systems support some kind of processor affinity command that you can use instead of these parameters to achieve the same affect.

6.6 PROCESSOR USAGE CHECKLIST

Table 6.1 summarizes processor-related configuration parameters and performance tips.

Table 6.1–Processor usage checklist

What to Check	How to Check	How to Alter
SPINCNT (INFORMIX-OnLine)	Check for **%idle** of processors with **vmstat, sar**; single CPU machines should have SPINCNT set to zero	SPINCNT configuration parameter
Parallel sorting (for multiprocessor systems)	Check for **%idle** of processors with **vmstat, sar**; check OnLine ready queue (INFORMIX-OnLine Dynamic Server) with **onstat -g rea**	Set (or unset) the PSORT_NPROCS environment variable
CPU vps (INFORMIX-OnLine Dynamic Server)	**onstat -g rea**	Increase dynamically by **onmode -p** or change NUMCPUVPS configuration parameter
MULTIPROCESSOR configuration parameter (INFORMIX-OnLine Dynamic Server)	**$ONCONFIG** file	Turn on (1) for multiprocessor machines; turn off (0) for single-processor machines
SINGLE_CPU_VP (INFORMIX-OnLine Dynamic Server)	**$ONCONFIG** file	Turn on (1) for single-processor machines; turn off (0) for multiprocessor machines
Processor Affinity (INFORMIX-OnLine Dynamic Server)		AFF_NPROCS, AFF_SPROC, or by an operating system command

Chapter 7

Query Performance

This chapter discusses techniques a database administrator may employ to improve query performance. The major topics discussed in this chapter follow:

- How the query optimizer works
- How indexes affect the optimizer
- What statistics are kept by the optimizer
- When the statistics are updated
- Viewing the query path
- How to influence the optimizer
- Decision support queries
- The OPTCOMPIND configuration parameters

7.1 HOW THE QUERY OPTIMIZER WORKS

The query optimizer is responsible for determining the best way to perform a specific query. It is generally *cost-based*, meaning the optimizer computes a cost for each query path and chooses the lowest cost path. A *query path* is simply a distinct method of executing a query that takes into account the order in which tables are read, how they are read (by an index or sequentially), and how they are joined with other tables in the query.

Join Methods

Before discussing the query optimizer further, it is important to understand how a query with more than one table can be executed. To join two tables, the database server must find a row that meets the query criteria in the first table and join it with the second table. The join consists of determining if a row in the second table meets the join filter criteria as well as other criteria in the query. For example, consider the following SELECT statement:

```
select * from customer,contact
   where customer.customer_num = contact.customer_num
      and customer.customer_num = 3020
```

The join filter between the two tables in the example is **customer.customer_num = contact.customer_num**. A row must be found in each table that has the same **customer_num** value. OnLine has a few choices in how the join between two tables is accomplished:

- **Nested loop join.** The nested loop join is a method where the first table is scanned for rows that meet the query criteria. Once a row is found in the first table, the database server searches for a corresponding row in the second table. Without indexes, the server would have to scan the first table once, and the second table x times where x is the number of rows that meet the query criteria in the first table. Fortunately, the optimizer usually chooses this method only if the second table has an index on the join column, so the entire second table does not have to be scanned once for each row found in the first table.

- **Sort merge join.** This join method is usually used when no index is available on the join column for both tables. Before the join begins, the database server sorts the rows from each table (after applying any query filters) on the join column. Once the rows are sorted, the algorithm for joining the two tables is easy. The database server simply reads both sorted tables sequentially.

- **Hash join.** The hash join is a join method that was added in INFORMIX-OnLine Dynamic Server in version 7.0. It is used when there are no indexes in one or both of the tables in the join and will usually replace the use of the sort merge join. One table is scanned and used to create a hash table. Using an internal hash function, each row is put in a "bucket" with other rows that have the same hash value. After the first table has been scanned and placed in a hash table, the second table is scanned once, and each row is looked up in the hash table to see if a join can be made. A hash join is usually faster than a sort merge join because no sort is required. However, there is some overhead in creating the hash table.

When join columns for both tables are indexed, the SELECT statement will most likely use the nested loop join unless there is a large amount of data in both tables to be read. The sort merge join has a high overhead in that rows from each table (or each table without an index) must be sorted. The hash join has the overhead of creating the initial hash table. However, the hash join is preferable when join columns for both tables are not indexed.

Optimizer Paths

Consider the following query:

```
select * from x,y,z where x.a = y.a and y.a = z.a
    and z.b = 30
```

The query would most likely be accomplished by one of the following methods (although all paths are examined!):

- Choose a row from table x. Then join the row with one or more rows in table y. Join the result with table z.
- Choose a row from table y. Then join the row with one or more rows in table x. Join the result with table z. (See Fig. 7.1.)
- Choose a row from table z. Then join the row with one or more rows in table y. Join the result with table x.

Figure 7.1-How tables are joined: an example

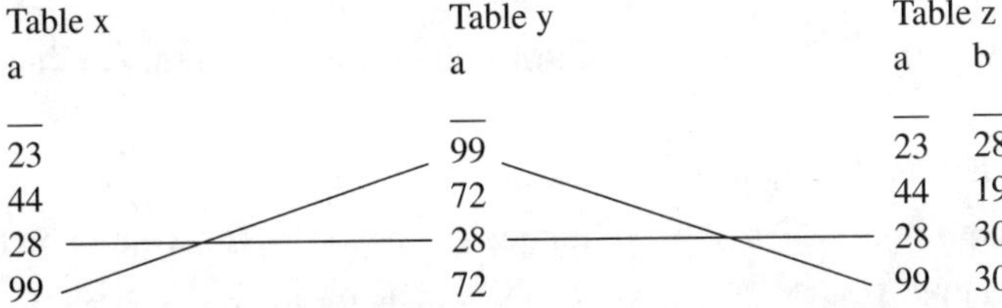

The order and the method in which the tables are read make up the query path. In determining the query path, usually the optimizer tries to eliminate as many rows as possible early in the query (although there are many other factors to consider). The smaller the number of rows that will fulfill the query from each table, the higher the probability that the table will be toward the front of the path. The number of rows that will fulfill the query for a table is known as the *table selectivity*. In the example, table z is probably the most selective because of the filter **z.b = 30**. Assuming that the tables are of equal size and **z.b** has an index, the optimizer will most likely choose the zyx path (path number three).

Note that the order of the tables in the query path is very important. For example, examining table x first and joining it with table y may be much better than examining table y first and joining it with table x.

7.2   INDEXES AND THE OPTIMIZER

The presence of indexes on filter columns in a SELECT statement profoundly affect the optimizer path and, eventually, the performance of a query. It would be wonderful to have an index on every column used as a filter in a query. However, the reality is that indexes take up disk space and adversely affect performance for INSERT, UPDATE, and DELETE statements. The administrator must balance SELECT performance with OLTP needs in deciding which columns to index.

As a minimum, you should index all primary and foreign keys in a database. Additionally, any columns that are used in important queries can be indexed as required.

7.3   OPTIMIZER STATISTICS

The optimizer uses statistics kept for a table to determine the selectivity. These statistics are kept in a series of system catalog tables (which are simply control tables kept with each database). The statistics kept for a table and its indexes follow:

- **systables.nrows**. The number of rows in the table.
- **systables.npused**. The number of pages used to store the data.
- **syscolumns.colmax**. The second largest value for a column (discarding the maximum value).
- **syscolumns.colmin**. The second smallest value for a column (discarding the minimum value).
- **sysindexes.leaves**. The number of leaf pages for the index.
- **sysindexes.nunique**. The number of unique values for the first column in the index.
- **sysindexes.clust**. How highly clustered the values for the first column in the index are.

Here's a simple example of how these statistics are used by the optimizer.

```
select * from customer where city = "LOS ANGELES" and
    customer_name = "ALVAREZ"
```

If the customer table has an index on both **city** and **customer_name**, which index should be used? Suppose the table has the following statistics:

```
systables.nrows = 1,000,000
sysindexes.nunique (for customer_name index) = 200000
sysindexes.nunique (for city index) = 100
```

Using these statistics, the optimizer can guess that there might be approximately 1,000,000/200,000 = 5 occurrences of "ALVAREZ" in the table and 1,000,000/100 = 100,000 customers that live in "LOS ANGELES" in the table. Given this simple calculation, the optimizer would most likely choose the **customer_name** index to retrieve the data. In reality, there are other statistics that the optimizer would analyze as well, such as the number of pages in each index and the number of levels of each b-tree.

The importance of these statistics is magnified when three or more tables are involved in a query.

Note that the optimizer cannot discern if the data within a table are skewed. Also, there is no information on unique values for columns that are not indexed (this deficiency is addressed in the INFORMIX-OnLine Dynamic Server data distributions feature addressed later in this chapter).

7.4 WHEN ARE THE STATISTICS UPDATED?

The statistics in the system catalog tables are not constantly updated. This type of behavior would be too costly to overall performance. Instead, the UPDATE STATISTICS statement refreshes the system catalog table statistics. You decide how often to run the UPDATE STATISTICS statement.

A disadvantage of running the UPDATE STATISTICS statement frequently is that it does incur some overhead because all index and data pages must be read to calculate the statistics. Since the pages are read into the buffer cache, you may see the overall read cache rate decrease while UPDATE STATISTICS is running. Also, when the statistics have been calculated, OnLine must briefly lock some rows in the system catalog tables to update the statistics. At the brief moment these columns are locked, other SQL statements needing to read these rows will receive errors.

It is very important to run UPDATE STATISTICS when the nature of the data in a table has changed significantly, especially after an initial load of data, or after a DELETE or UPDATE that affects a large number of rows. You can update the statistics for one table.

```
UPDATE STATISTICS FOR table
```

You can update the statistics for an entire database.

```
UPDATE STATISTICS
```

You may consider embedding UPDATE STATISTICS in an application process that runs nightly or weekly in a period of slow activity.

7.5 VIEWING THE QUERY PATH

You can record the path the optimizer chooses for a query by running SET EXPLAIN ON before the query is optimized. SET EXPLAIN ON places the query plan in a file in your current directory, called **sqexplain.out**. A sample query plan follows:

```
QUERY:
------
select * from orders, items where orders.order_num =
     items.order_num

Estimated Cost: 11
Estimated # of Rows Returned: 67

1) informix.orders: SEQUENTIAL SCAN

2) informix.items: INDEX PATH

(1) Index Keys: order_num
Lower Index Filter: informix.items.order_num =
     informix.orders.order_num
```

The query plan output is valuable for determining if the query is running optimally. Some of the things you can notice about the query plan output are

- **The estimated cost of a query.** This value is to compare how "expensive" one path is compared to another. The estimated cost cannot really translate to the amount of time the query will take.

- **The estimated number of rows returned by a query.** This value will tend to be a very rough estimate, and will be more accurate if all filter columns have indexes and if data distributions (an INFORMIX-OnLine Dynamic Server feature explained later in this chapter) were created on all filter columns.

- **The order of the tables in the query plan.** In the example, the **orders** table is read first, followed by the **items** table. In many cases, the optimizer chooses the table with the fewest number of rows that will be selected by the query.

- **How each table will be read.** In the example, the **orders** table will be read sequentially and an index path used for **items**. This is the usual method for a nested loop join when the first table has no filter.

- **What indexes will be used for an index scan.**

- **The type of join method used.** If the query path does not mention the join method, the nested loop join will be used. If the sort merge join will be used, you will see something like:

```
1) informix.items: SEQUENTIAL SCAN

SORT SCAN: informix.items.order_num

2) informix.orders: SEQUENTIAL SCAN

SORT SCAN: informix.orders.order_num
```

```
MERGE JOIN
          Merge Filters: informix.orders.order_num =
                              informix.items.order_num
```

7.6   CASE STUDY 1

A user complains about the response time of a query. After getting the details about the query, you run and time the query yourself. It takes 2 minutes to run.

You turn SET EXPLAIN ON and run the query with the parameters the user was running with. The SET EXPLAIN OUTPUT is

```
QUERY:
------
select * from account,transaction,teller
where account.account_nbr = transaction.account_nbr
and transaction.teller_num = teller.teller_num
and teller.teller_num = 22

Estimated Cost: 46054
Estimated # of Rows Returned: 209

1) informix.transaction: SEQUENTIAL SCAN

2) informix.teller: INDEX PATH
    Filters: informix.teller.teller_num = 22

   (1) Index Keys: teller_num
          Lower Index Filter: informix.teller.teller_num =
       informix.transaction.teller_num

3) informix.account: INDEX PATH

        (1) Index Keys: account_nbr
        Lower Index Filter: informix.account.account_nbr =
       informix.transaction.account_nbr
```

By looking at the SET EXPLAIN output, you notice the sequential scan of the **transaction** table. This operation is probably what is taking the majority of the 2 minutes to run the query.

You use DB-Access to find the number of rows in each table. The **account** and **transaction** tables have approximately the same number of rows: about 30,000. The **teller** table has only 100 entries. By running a few quick SELECT statements, you note that the **teller** table has only one row where **teller_num = 22**. The **transaction** table is first in the query path because it does not have an index on **teller_num**. By putting the **transaction** table first in the query path, the optimizer avoids putting an index on **teller_num** or using a sort merge to join the **teller** and **transaction** tables.

After some thought about the consequences, you decide to put an index on **transaction.teller_num**. By adding another index, you realize that the INSERT, UPDATE, and DELETE operations on the transaction table may suffer slightly.

After adding the index, the query now runs in 5 seconds. The SET EXPLAIN output is

```
QUERY:
------
select * from account,transaction,teller
where account.account_nbr = transaction.account_nbr
and transaction.teller_num = teller.teller_num
and teller.teller_num = 22

Estimated Cost: 111
Estimated # of Rows Returned: 10

1) informix.teller: INDEX PATH

(1) Index Keys: teller_num
Lower Index Filter: informix.teller.teller_num = 22
2) informix.transaction: INDEX PATH

(1) Index Keys: branch_nbr
 Lower Index Filter: informix.transaction.teller_num =
        informix.teller.teller_num

3) informix.account: INDEX PATH

(1) Index Keys: account_nbr
Lower Index Filter: informix.account.account_nbr =
        informix.transaction.account_nbr
```

You notice now that the **teller** table is first in the query path, because it is the smaller table and can be joined with **transaction** using an index.

7.7 INFLUENCING THE OPTIMIZER WITH SET OPTIMIZATION LOW

The thoroughness of the optimizer in examining all paths can actually increase the total amount of time the query takes. The optimization time is insignificant for queries involving only a few tables. However, for SELECT statements with more than four or five tables, the number of paths the optimizer must examine increase dramatically, along with the optimization time.

The SET OPTIMIZATION LOW statement, executed before the SELECT statement is optimized, reduces some of the work the optimizer does by eliminating unlikely paths.

Let's use a SELECT statement with four tables as an example of how SET OPTIMIZATION LOW reduces optimization work:

```
select * from w,x,y,z where x.a = y.a and y.b = z.b
      and x.b = w.b
```

First, the optimizer computes a cost for all two-way joins in the query, such as the xy join, the yz join, the xw join, the zy join (order is important!), and so on. The two-way join with the lowest cost is kept, and all other further paths involving the other two-way joins are discarded by the optimizer. For example, if the yz join is the lowest cost, the optimizer would examine costs only for the possible three-way joins that start with the yz join (i.e., yzx and yzw). See Figure 7.2.

Figure 7.2-Optimizer paths with SET OPTIMIZATION LOW

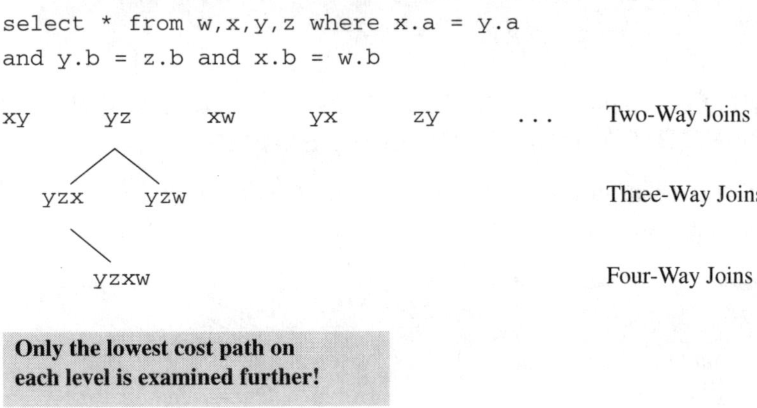

The advantages of SET OPTIMIZATION LOW is that the optimization process will run faster for a query involving more than a few tables, because of the vastly reduced number of paths that must be examined. The disadvantage is that the optimizer might inadvertently discard the lowest cost path early in the analysis, causing the overall query performance to decrease! That is why you should use SET OPTIMIZATION LOW with care.

Here are some guidelines for deciding when to use SET OPTIMIZATION LOW:

1. Consider using only SET OPTIMIZATION LOW if the query has more than four tables.

2. Run and time the query using production data.

3. Obtain the query path by running the query with SET EXPLAIN ON.

4. Obtain the query path by running the query with SET OPTIMIZATION LOW and SET EXPLAIN ON. Is the query path the same as in step 3? If so, then the optimizer chose the correct path while keeping optimization time to a minimum. Continue to step 5.

5. Rerun and time the query using SET OPTIMIZATION LOW. If the query time is significantly faster, then SET OPTIMIZATION LOW will positively affect your performance!

To use SET OPTIMIZATION LOW for a specific query, place the SET OPTIMIZA-TION LOW statement immediately before the query and SET OPTIMIZATION HIGH after the query. The SET OPTIMIZATION HIGH statement instructs the optimizer to perform a full cost analysis (the default) for queries following. For example,

```
SET OPTIMIZATION LOW
SELECT * FROM ......
SET OPTIMIZATION HIGH
```

7.8 INFLUENCING THE OPTIMIZER WITH DATA DISTRIBUTIONS (INFORMIX-OnLine Dynamic Server)

The statistics in **systables**, **syscolumns**, or **sysindexes** do not take into account any skewed data in the table. In the example SELECT statement used earlier,

```
select * from customer where city = "LOS ANGELES" and
    customer_name = "ALVAREZ"
```

How would the query optimizer know if the **customer** table held only one customer from the city of Los Angeles? Would the optimizer be able to discern that most of the customers in the **customer** table live in Los Angeles?

The effect of skewed data on an optimizer's ability to pick the correct query path will be magnified as more and larger tables are involved in a query.

The optimizer uses *data distributions* to detect skewed data and also to provide more information on nonindexed columns.

A distribution can be created on each column. To create a distribution, the table is divided into pieces, or "bins." Each of the bins describe an approximately equal number of rows except for the last bin, which might describe fewer rows than the other bins. Then statistics are gathered and stored for each of these bins. The following information is known for each bin:

- The first and last value represented by the bin,
- The number of unique values in each bin, and
- For the last bin, the number of rows represented by the bin.

In addition to statistics kept on each of the bins, information is also kept on any value with a large number of duplicates. To qualify as "highly duplicate," the value must have more duplicates than one-fourth the number of rows in a bin. The highly duplicate values are excluded from the statistics in the individual bins. For each highly duplicate value, the following information is kept:

- The highly duplicate column value and
- The number of rows containing the column value.

The statistics kept for each bin and for the duplicate are stored, encoded, in a system catalog table called **sysdistrib**.

Generating a Distribution

To generate a distribution for a column, use the UPDATE STATISTICS statement. You can run the statement for every column in the database, for every column in a table, or for an individual column in a table. You can also choose to sample rows or create a distribution on all of the actual rows. Sampling rows for a distribution is called MEDIUM mode. Using all rows in the table for the distribution is called HIGH mode.

Some examples follow:

- Create a distribution on a column using sampling (MEDIUM).

```
UPDATE STATISTICS MEDIUM FOR TABLE table(column)
```

- Create a distribution on all columns in a table using actual rows (HIGH).

```
UPDATE STATISTICS HIGH FOR TABLE table
```

- Create a distribution on all columns in a database using sampling.

```
UPDATE STATISTICS MEDIUM
```

Displaying a Column Distribution

You can see a column's distribution with the **dbschema** utility, using the **-hd** option.

```
dbschema -d database -hd table
```

A portion of the output of **dbschema** for one column's distribution follows:

```
Distribution for informix.transaction.account_nbr

Constructed on 05/22/1994

High Mode, 0.500000 Resolution

--- DISTRIBUTION ---

 ( 1)
 1: (  460,  75,   75)
 2: (  460,  76,  151)
 3: (  460,  74,  226)
 4: (  460,  76,  302)
 5: (  460,  79,  381)
 6: (  460,  71,  452)
 7: (  460,  74,  526)
 8: (  460,  73,  599)
 9: (  460,  78,  677)
10: (  460,  79,  757)
```

The statistics for each bin are shown on one line. The first column shows the number of rows represented by the bin. The next column shows the number of unique values in the bin. The last column shows the high value represented by the bin. In the example, bin 1 represents values from 1 to 75. Bin 2 represents values from 76 to 151.

Adjusting the Accuracy of the Statistics

You can increase the chance of accounting for all skewed data by simply increasing the number of "bins" in the distribution. By increasing the number of bins, you are decreasing the number of rows that are described in one set of statistics. You are also changing the definition of *highly duplicate* (remember that a highly duplicate value has >25% of the number of rows for one bin).

As an example, suppose that you create a distribution on a column, such as **city**, for a table that holds 10,000 rows. You start out with 10 bins, which means that each bin holds approximately 10,000/10 = 1000 rows. The distribution might be created as shown in Figure 7.3 (only four bins are shown).

In bin 1, 20 unique values are represented. The optimizer will assume that they are equally distributed and project that there are 1000/20 = 50 duplicate rows for each value between "Atlanta" and "Chicago."

Now let's say that you increase the number of bins to 100 and re-create the distribution. Now each bin represents 10,000/100 = 100 rows. The distribution might look something like Figure 7.4.

Figure 7.3-Distribution when data held in 10 bins

Atlanta- Chicago	Columbus- Dresden	Dublin- Hong Kong	Houston- Los Angeles	· · ·
Bin 1: Unique: 20	Bin 2: Unique: 15	Bin 3: Unique: 3	Bin 4: Unique: 10	

Figure 7.4-Distribution when data held in 100 bins

Atlanta- Bangkok	Columbus- Chicago	Cincinnati- Dresden	Dublin- Hong Kong	· · ·
Bin 1: Unique: 5	Bin 2: Unique: 15	Bin 3: Unique: 3	Bin 4: Unique: 10	

In bin 1, there are now five unique values represented. The optimizer will now project that there are 100/5 = 20 duplicates for every value between "Atlanta" and "Bangkok."

You can adjust the number of bins in the UPDATE STATISTICS statement using the RESOLUTION clause. A RESOLUTION of 1 means that 1% of the data will be represented by a bin, and there will be 100 bins. For example,

```
UPDATE STATISTICS MEDIUM ON table RESOLUTION 1
```

Finally, if you choose to create a distribution using a sample (MEDIUM), you can control how big a sample is used, with the combination of RESOLUTION and another value called CONFIDENCE. CONFIDENCE is a statistical measure of the reliability of the sample. As CONFIDENCE increases (up to .99) and the RESOLUTION value decreases (the number of bins increase), the sample size increases. To alter the CONFIDENCE from its default value of .95, include the clause in the UPDATE STATISTICS statement. For example:

```
UPDATE STATISTICS MEDIUM ON table RESOLUTION .1 CONFIDENCE .99
```

Generally, you do not have to adjust the CONFIDENCE from its default value.

So What Do I Do with These Distributions?

If you are happy with your query performance (who is?), don't bother with distributions. They involve some overhead to gather and create the distribution—reading and sorting the rows, creating the distribution, and storing it.

However, if your goal is ever-increasing performance and you can afford the overhead of creating distributions, you should run UPDATE STATISTICS MEDIUM on all columns that might possibly be used as a filter in a query. You can run UPDATE STATISTICS HIGH for columns with an index, because the presence of an index means that the column values won't have to be sorted for the distribution.

If, after creating distributions with this strategy, a query is still running poorly, follow these steps:

1. Run and time the query using production data.
2. Run the query with SET EXPLAIN ON to get the query path.
3. Run UPDATE STATISTICS HIGH on all columns involved as filters in the query.
4. Rerun and time the query.
5. Run the query with SET EXPLAIN ON.
6. If the query path is the same for steps 2 and 5, UPDATE STATISTICS HIGH will not affect the query. If the query path did change and the query time in step 4 is better than in step 1, UPDATE STATISTICS HIGH on the filter columns will positively affect performance!

7.9 DECISION SUPPORT QUERIES

Decision support queries are queries that must read and process a large amount of data. Often, these queries have ORDER BY, SUM, GROUP BY, or some other clause that requires more processing.

Decision support queries do not necessarily benefit from indexes on columns. When reading a large amount of the table, it is probably more efficient to scan the entire table rather than reading down an index b-tree.

Decision support queries benefit most from using Parallel Data Query, discussed in chapter 10. This feature should be used on multiprocessor systems where table sizes are relatively large.

7.10 OPTCOMPIND (INFORMIX-ONLINE DYNAMIC SERVER)

OPTCOMPIND is a configuration parameter and environment variable that can influence how the optimizer reacts. It is available in INFORMIX-OnLine Dynamic Server releases starting with 7.0. The best way to define how the OPTCOMPIND parameter is used is with an example. Suppose that you have two tables, A and B. You also have an index on B.x. You execute the following query:

```
select * from A, B where A.x = B.x;
```

How this query will be optimized depends upon the value of OPTCOMPIND:

- OPTCOMPIND is 0. Consider only the index join, or scan, using the index on B.x.
- OPTCOMPIND is 1. If the transaction is in Repeatable Read mode, then consider only the index join, or scan, using the index on B.x; otherwise, choose the lowest cost join, or scan, method.
- OPTCOMPIND is 2. Choose the lowest cost between the table (scan, index) or join (index, hash, and sort merge).

The default setting of OPTCOMPIND=2, in conjunction with data distributions, will usually produce the better path. This is especially evident in decision support queries where a large amount of data must be read and using an index is not efficient.

The following example shows how OPTCOMPIND affects an actual query. Before running this query, UPDATE STATISTICS HIGH was executed and OPTCOMPIND was set to 0.

```
QUERY:
------
SELECT *
  FROM customer,orders,items
    WHERE orders.customer_num = customer.customer_num
      AND orders.order_num = items.order_num

Estimated Cost: 20
Estimated # of Rows Returned: 50

1) informix.orders: SEQUENTIAL SCAN

2) informix.customer: INDEX PATH

  (1) Index Keys: customer_num
  Lower Index Filter: informix.customer.customer_num
     =informix.orders.customer_num

3) informix.items: INDEX PATH
    (1) Index Keys: order_num
     Lower Index Filter: informix.items.order_num
    =informix.orders.order_num
```

Notice that the optimizer chose the index path on the second table in the join pair (customer in the orders-customer pair and items in the orders/customer result-items pair). That fits the original definition of how OPTCOMPIND affects queries perfectly. Notice that a nested loop join was performed for both pairs.

Next, OPTCOMPIND is set to 2 and the same query is run with SET EXPLAIN ON.

```
SELECT *
  FROM customer,orders,items
    WHERE orders.customer_num = customer.customer_num
    AND orders.order_num = items.order_num

Estimated Cost: 12
Estimated # of Rows Returned: 50
1) informix.orders: SEQUENTIAL SCAN

2) informix.customer: SEQUENTIAL SCAN

  DYNAMIC HASH JOIN (Build Outer)
  Dynamic Hash Filters: informix.orders.customer_num
     =informix.customer.customer_num
3) informix.items: SEQUENTIAL SCAN

  DYNAMIC HASH JOIN (Build Outer)
   Dynamic Hash Filters: informix.orders.order_num
      =informix.items.order_num
```

Notice that the optimizer found that the lowest cost method was *not* to use indexes and just read the tables sequentially. This makes sense in our example, because these tables are small and also all rows in each table are being read.

Since no index is involved, a hash join is being used to join these tables. An interesting side bar to this discussion is that you may see an increase in the amount of temporary space (memory and disk) if you set OPTCOMPIND to 2, because decision support queries may bypass existing indexes to use the lower costing scan and hash joins.

Also, another interesting note is that OnLine builds the hash table on the second table listed. However, if the key words "Build Outer" are listed, this means that the hash table is built on the first table listed.

7.11 IF ALL ELSE FAILS...

Sometimes, despite your efforts to index the appropriate columns and run UPDATE STA-TISTICS properly, you deduce from the SET EXPLAIN output that the optimizer is still choosing an incorrect path for a particular query, which adversely affects performance. Many an administrator has dreamed of having an optimizer override feature for these particular queries.

If all the previous advice has not achieved what you think the optimal query path should be, sometimes a few "tricks" can affect the optimizer's cost calculations enough to get the results you want. Some of these tricks follow:

- Index (or don't index) columns in small tables. As a rule, you usually want to index primary and foreign keys of all tables, regardless of the table size. The optimizer can then decide whether to use the index or read the table sequentially. However, by adding or dropping an index on these smaller tables, you can sometimes affect the query path positively.

- Run SET OPTIMIZATION LOW, even for queries with less than five tables. Sometimes the change in paths that the optimizer examines may positively affect the final choice in query path.

- Alter the order of tables in the SELECT statement. Even though the order of tables in a query is not supposed to be significant, sometimes the order may matter if tables are similar in size and the optimizer costs are similar between two-way joins.

- Add extra, nonmeaningful filters. Sometimes you can influence the optimizer by adding a filter in the WHERE clause. For example, a query can be rewritten from

```
SELECT * from a,b,c where a.x = b.x and b.y = c.y
    where a.y = 20 and c.z = 30
```

to something like this:

```
SELECT * from a,b,c where a.x = b.x and b.y = c.y
    where a.y = 20 and c.z = 30 and c.y > 0
```

Extra filters may give the optimizer incentive to choose the table earlier in the query path.

7.12 CASE STUDY 2 (USING DISTRIBUTIONS)

The user complains of a slow response from a particular query, especially for the companies most often queried region, region 10000. You extract the actual SQL from the application, replace the variables with the values that the user was running with, and time the query:

```
time dbaccess db1 query.sql >outfile 2>outerr
```

The elapsed time is 10.8 seconds. Next, you execute SET EXPLAIN ON and rerun the query. The SET EXPLAIN output shows:

```
QUERY:
------
select * from account,store where account.region = 10000
   and store.location = 105
   and account.account_nbr = store.account_nbr
```

```
Estimated Cost: 77
Estimated # of Rows Returned: 1

1) informix.account: INDEX PATH

    (1) Index Keys: region
          Lower Index Filter: informix.account.region = 10000

2) informix.store: INDEX PATH

  Filters: informix.store.location = 105

  (1) Index Keys: account_nbr
          Lower Index Filter: informix.store.account_nbr =
      informix.account.account_nbr
```

You first check that both tables are read with an index, evident by the INDEX PATH designation. You notice that the **account** table is chosen first in the path. Is this the optimal path? You run the following queries:

```
select count(*) from account where region = 10000
select count(*) from store where location = 105
```

The first SELECT returns 10,000 rows. The second SELECT returns 105 rows. Since the optimal path is usually one that eliminates as many rows as possible early in the query, it seems that in this case the **store** table should have been first in the query path. You wonder why the optimizer chose the path it did and check the statistics for the table, filter columns, and indexes for the filter columns.

```
select * from systables, syscolumns, sysindexes where
   syscolumns.colname = "region" and
   syscolumns.colno = sysindexes.part1 and
   sysindexes.tabid = systables.tabid and
   systables.tabname = "account"

select * from systables, syscolumns, sysindexes where
   syscolumns.colname = "location" and
   syscolumns.colno = sysindexes.part1 and
   sysindexes.tabid = systables.tabid and
   systables.tabname = "store"
```

You notice in the statistics listed by the SELECT statement that, for the **region** column, the **nunique** (number of unique values) statistic shows 1002. Since there are 11,000 rows in the **account** table, the number of duplicate rows projected per value is 11,000/1,002 = ~11. For the **location** column, the **nunique** statistic shows 111. Since there are 11,000 rows in the **store** table as well, the number of duplicates projected by the optimizer is 11,000/111 = ~100. The optimizer chose the correct path according to these statistics, assuming that approximately 11 rows would be chosen from the **account** table to join to the values in the **store** table.

The reality is that 1000 rows were selected from the account table! This is a classic example of skewed data. The optimizer cannot discern skewed data without using data distributions. So you decide to create distributions for the **region**, **account_nbr**, and **location** columns. Since these columns all have indexes, you run UPDATE STATISTICS in HIGH mode.

```
update statistics high for table account(region);
update statistics high for table account(account_nbr);
update statistics high for table store(location);
update statistics high for table store(account_nbr);
```

Next, you rerun the query with SET EXPLAIN ON. The **sqexplain.out** file shows:

```
QUERY:
------
select * from account,store where region = 10000
   and location = 105
   and account.account_nbr = store.account_nbr

Estimated Cost: 170
Estimated # of Rows Returned: 9

1) informix.store: INDEX PATH

  (1)      Index Keys: location
           Lower Index Filter: informix.store.location = 105

2) informix.account: INDEX PATH

 Filters: informix.account.region = 10000

  (1)      Index Keys: account_nbr
           Lower Index Filter: informix.account.account_nbr =
       informix.store.account_nbr
```

From this output, you see that the query path has changed to SELECT first from the **store** table and join with the **account** table.

You then time the query again and find that, indeed, the change in query path has resulted in the query running several seconds faster. Although the gap in times between the two queries is small, it will become even more noticeable as both tables grow.

7.13 CHECKLIST FOR POORLY PERFORMING QUERIES

Table 7.1 summarizes the actions an administrator can take to improve query performance.

Table 7.1–Checklist for poorly performing queries

What to Check	How to Check	How to Alter
Has UPDATE STATISTICS been run?	Look for statistics entries in the **systables**, **syscolumns**, and **sysindexes** tables	UPDATE STATISTICS
Are filter columns in the SELECT statement indexed?	**dbschema -d** *database*	CREATE INDEX
Try SET OPTIMIZATION LOW for queries with > 4 tables		SET OPTIMIZATION LOW must be run before the query is optimized
Create distributions on filter columns	**dbschema -d** *database* **-hd**	UPDATE STATISTICS MEDIUM or UPDATE STATISTICS HIGH

Chapter 8

Locking and Performance

The way locking is handled by applications can substantially affect the overall performance of an OnLine system. The potentially negative effect locking can have makes it an important area for the administrator to monitor. The administrator should audit application development processes to make sure that potentially damaging practices are avoided and the most efficient locking method is used. The major topics discussed in this chapter follow:

- How locks work
- Lock levels
- Lock types
- Locking duration
- Locking recommendations
- Lock monitoring

8.1 HOW LOCKS WORK

Locks are used for *concurrency control*, or protecting one user's work from another. For example, when a row is updated, no other user should be able to change the row until the transaction that updates the row is committed. Even other readers should not be able to view the row until it is committed, because the change could be rolled back at any time during the transaction.

When a lock is placed on an item in a database, the item itself is not altered in any way. Instead, the locks are placed in a lock table, a structure in shared memory (see Fig. 8.1).

Figure 8.1-The lock table

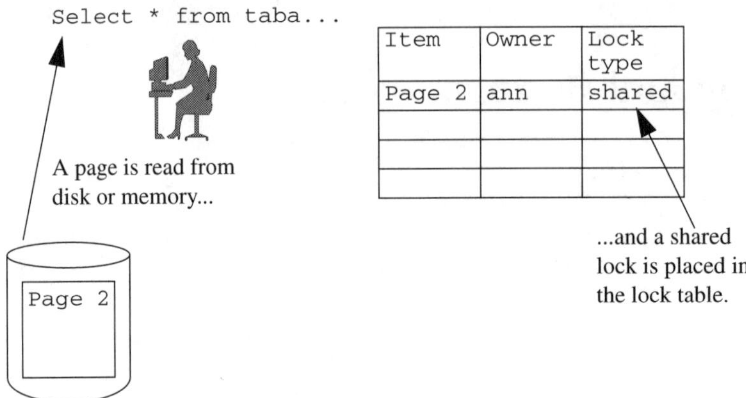

When another user must access or update an item, the user must first check the lock table to see if the lock exists there. If it does, the user will receive an error. Otherwise, if SET LOCK MODE TO WAIT is set in the application, the user will wait until the lock is released.

Locks are not only placed on data but on indexes as well. When you update a row in a table that has two indexes, you will probably place at least three locks, one for the row and one for each index key.

The administrator can specify, up to the system limit of 256,000, the number of locks that can be placed at any one time by all users (sessions) in the OnLine system. The configuration parameter that controls the size of the lock table is called LOCKS. If all users collectively require more locks than are specified by this parameter, the operations requesting the locks will fail. You can monitor if the LOCKS parameter is exceeded by running **onstat -p** (or, for INFORMIX-OnLine, **tbstat -p**). In the following sample **-p** output (only a portion of the output is shown), the LOCKS value was exceeded five times.

```
ovtbls   ovlock   ovuserthread   ovbuff   usercpu   syscpu   numckpts   flushes
0        5        0              0        45.47     60.05    2          1042
```

The **ovlock** field in this output increments every time a user requests a lock and can't get one because the LOCKS parameter is exceeded.

8.2 LOCK LEVELS

Four basic lock levels can be applied in an OnLine system:

- **Database locks.** Database locks prevent other users from adding or updating rows in any table or altering the structure of any table in the database. A database lock is placed by adding the EXCLUSIVE keyword to the DATABASE statement:

```
DATABASE dbname EXCLUSIVE
```

- **Table locks.** Table locks prevent other users from adding or updating rows in a specific table in the database. A table lock is placed by executing a LOCK TABLE statement in one of two forms. The first method shown here will allow other users to SELECT from rows in the table but disallow any INSERT, UPDATE, or DELETE activity. The second method, with the IN EXCLUSIVE MODE clause shown next, disallows both update and most query activity (except for a specific execution of SELECT statement called *dirty reads* that do not check for locks).

```
LOCK TABLE tabname
LOCK TABLE tabname IN EXCLUSIVE MODE
```

- **Page locks.** Page locks protect all rows or index items on a single data or index page.
- **Row locks.** Row locks protect only specific rows or index keys.

When a table is created, you specify whether the table will use row locks or page locks. If the DATABASE EXCLUSIVE or LOCK TABLE statements are not explicitly executed, the SQL statements run by a user will follow the locking mechanism (page or row) specified by the table.

To create a table with row locking, use the LOCK MODE ROW clause, as shown here:

```
CREATE TABLE tabname(col1 integer,...) LOCK MODE ROW;
```

Page locking is the default method of locking. To create a table with page locking, omit the LOCK MODE clause or use the LOCK MODE PAGE option:

```
CREATE TABLE tabname(col1 integer,...) LOCK MODE PAGE;
```

After the table is created, you can alter the lock level with the ALTER TABLE statement.

```
ALTER TABLE tabname LOCK MODE (ROW)
```

To determine if a table has row or page locking, look at the entry for the table in the system catalog table, **systables**.

```
select locklevel from systables
    where tabname = "tabname";
```

A lock level of "P" means the table has page locking. A lock level of "R" means the table has row locking.

8.3　LOCK TYPES

Generally, four types of locks can be put on a row or page. The type of lock held determines the amount of concurrency control on an item.

- **Shared locks.** Shared locks allow other users to read an item but not to update it. Multiple shared locks can be placed on the same row. A user might want to place a shared lock on a row while it is being read to keep other users from changing the row's value.

- **Exclusive locks.** Exclusive locks prevent other users from reading or updating the row. Exclusive locks are used when a row is INSERTed, UPDATEd, or DELETEd.

- **Update locks.** Update locks are used when you fetch a row with an update cursor in an application. It is similar to a shared lock, except that it is *promotable* to an exclusive lock once the UPDATE actually occurs.

- **Intent locks.** Intent locks are placed at the table or database level and prevent actions from occurring at the table level while users are executing operations at the row or page level. For example, if a user UPDATEs a row, you will see a lock placed at the row level as well as an intent lock placed at the table level.

Table 8.1 shows which locks are allowed on an item by another user if the first user already holds a lock on the same item. For example, if user 1 holds an exclusive lock on an item, no other lock is allowed by user 2 on the same item. However, if user 1 holds a shared lock on an item, user 2 can hold either a shared lock or an update lock on the item at the same time.

Table 8.1–Lock Interaction

		User 2 Requests		
		Exclusive Lock	Shared Lock	Update Lock
User 1 Holds	Exclusive Lock	Not allowed	Not allowed	Not allowed
	Shared Lock	Not allowed	Allowed	Allowed
	Update Lock	Not allowed	Allowed	Not allowed

8.4　LOCK DURATION FOR INSERT, UPDATE, OR DELETE

When an UPDATE, INSERT, or DELETE statement places an exclusive lock on an item, how long it is held depends on the logging mode of the database and the type of transaction logic used in the application.

Databases without logging release locks immediately after the operation has completed.

Databases with logging use transaction logic to control lock duration. In many applications, SQL statements are part of a *transaction*; that is, statements that must be completed entirely or not at all. A transaction starts with a BEGIN WORK statement and completes with a COMMIT WORK statement for successful transactions, or a ROLLBACK WORK statement for unsuccessful transactions. A simple example of a transaction without the error-checking logic follows:

```
begin work;
insert into tab1 values (...);        {Lock placed here}
update tab2 set x = x +1              {Lock(s) placed here}
      where x > 20;
commit work;                          {All locks released}
```

In this transaction, one row will be inserted into **tab1**, and one or more rows in **tab2** will be updated. The exclusive locks placed on each of the rows updated in **tab2** and the new row in **tab1** *remain until the end of the transaction*.

In some cases, a single SQL statement is not embedded between the BEGIN WORK or COMMIT WORK statement. In these cases, the SQL statement forms its own, or a *singleton*, transaction, and the COMMIT WORK is implied after the statement. In singleton transactions, the locks *remain until the end of the statement*.

8.5   LOCK DURATION FOR SELECT STATEMENTS—ISOLATION LEVELS

The lock duration for SELECT statements are determined by the type of *isolation level* used within an application. There are four isolation levels for SELECT statements:

- **Dirty read.** The dirty read isolation level means that all locks are ignored by the SELECT statement, and no locks are placed on any rows that are read. If a database is not logged, all applications will read data with the dirty read isolation level. Dirty read is the most efficient isolation level. However, applications face the possibility of reading rows that have been added or changed by another user but not committed. These uncommitted rows could possibly be "rolled back" (changed back to their previous values or deleted) after being read by an application using dirty read.

- **Committed read.** The committed read isolation level means that each row fetched by a SELECT statement will be tested for the presence of a lock. If an exclusive lock is held by another user on the row or page, the FETCH or SELECT statement will receive an error. If SET LOCK MODE TO WAIT is set in the application, the application will wait until the lock has been released. Note that once the row is tested for locks, other users can then immediately place a lock on the row without the original reader knowing. This isolation level is the default for all logged databases.

- **Cursor stability.** As the name implies, the cursor stability isolation level keeps the contents of the row stable the entire time the row is being examined in the application. It prevents the current row from being exclusively locked by another user by placing a shared lock on the item until the next row is fetched or the cursor is closed in the application.

- **Repeatable read.** The repeatable read isolation level acquires a shared lock on every row examined by the SELECT statement. The shared locks are all held *until the end of the transaction*. This isolation level is often used by applications that cannot have new or updated rows in the set of information being read. For example, an application trying to obtain an account balance might need to make sure that new transactions are not being added while the account balance is being calculated. The repeatable read isolation level can potentially lock many rows, as even rows that are examined but not returned to the application are locked. This isolation level is the default isolation level of ANSI databases.

You change the isolation level from the default within an application by using the SET ISOLATION statement, for example:

```
SET ISOLATION TO CURSOR STABILITY
```

Applications accessing databases without logging cannot use the SET ISOLATION statement; only the dirty read isolation level will be used.

8.6   USING LOCKS EFFICIENTLY

How locks are used can affect the performance of the entire OnLine system. The database or system administrator should periodically monitor how the applications are using locks.

The goal in lock usage is to get the correct amount of concurrency control while:

- **Minimizing the number of items locked.** The more locks that are placed by one user, the higher the probability that other users must wait until these locks are released before continuing work.

- **Minimizing how long the items are locked.** The locks should only be held as long as necessary to obtain the correct amount of concurrency.

Here are some recommendations for using locks efficiently.

Avoid Using the Repeatable Read Isolation Level

The repeatable read isolation level potentially places locks on more items, and for a longer period of time, than the other isolation levels. Unless the application requires the use of repeatable read, avoid it. Remember that repeatable read is the default isolation level for databases created in ANSI mode.

Create Tables with Row-Level Locking

Row-level locking increases concurrency because the database server is locking the smallest-granularity item possible. *Page locking* means that even if only one row is being updated, all the rows on the page are unavailable. A table with a small row size can pack 50–100 rows on a single page. Index pages are even more dense; updating a key value for a table using page locking may lock 200 other key values!

Page-level locking should be used for tables that are usually updated with batch processes. When large numbers of rows are being UPDATEd or INSERTed at one time, only one page lock is placed for multiple rows. Using page locks may be the only way to avoid the 256,000 limit on the number of locks in the OnLine system.

Remember that page-level locking is the default locking level when a table is created, and you must specifically request row-level locking with the LOCK MODE ROW clause.

Use Dirty Read for Noncritical Applications

The dirty read isolation level means that no locks are placed or checked. An application will receive slightly better performance when dirty read is used. A common use for dirty read is in reports where reading uncommitted rows is acceptable. Also, nonvolatile tables are a good candidate for dirty read.

Keep Transactions Short to Avoid Concurrency Problems

Since locks are released at the end of the transaction, it makes sense to complete a transaction as quickly as possible. Keep interactive statements (statements that wait for input from a user) out of transaction logic if possible. Put only required logic between the BEGIN WORK and COMMIT WORK statements.

If possible, avoid transactions that update a large number of rows. Besides posing a concurrency problem, the transaction may become a *long transaction*. A long transaction is one that spans a certain percentage of logical logs—the percentage is specified by the LTXHWM configuration parameter. Long transactions will automatically be rolled back by the database server. Long transactions are a waste of resources, both the database server resources to roll back the transaction, and the lock resources that are not released until the transaction is rolled back.

If Possible, Lock the Table for Large Update Operations

The LOCK TABLE statement using the IN EXCLUSIVE MODE option places only one lock on the table, versus one lock for each row with row-level locking. By locking the table, you reduce the number of locks that are placed, resulting in slightly better performance. You also guard against the possibility that the transaction will fail because it reaches the maximum number of locks available in the OnLine system. Although LOCK TABLE reduces the availability of the table to other users, it enables a large update operation to be completed faster.

8.7   MONITORING LOCK USAGE

The administrator should suspect lock problems when specific applications are hung for short periods of time. By monitoring locks, you can see how many locks are held by each user as well as exactly what is being locked.

Monitoring Lock Usage with INFORMIX-OnLine

The administrator can get a good idea of how often a user must wait for another user to release a lock with the **tbstat -p** command. The output of this command has a **lokwaits** column, which is incremented every time a user waits for a lock.

```
bufwaits lokwaits lockreqs deadlks dltouts lchwaits ckpwaits compress
13707    22       28175128 0       0       123442   1        65
```

In the preceding output, users had to wait for a lock to be released 22 times. You should monitor this value to see if it gets unusually high. If it does, you must monitor individual users and the number and type of locks they are holding.

To see exactly what locks are held, use the **tbstat -k** command. Here is a sample **tbstat -k** report:

```
Locks
address   wtlist  owner     lklist    type     tblsnum   rowid  size
10004ed8  0       10001cf8  0         HDR+X    1000002   207    0
10004f18  0       10001cf8  10004f78  HDR+IX   1000095   0      0
10004f58  0       10001cf8  10004f18  HDR+X    1000095   101    0
10004f78  0       10001cf8  10004ed8  HDR+S    1000002   208    0
10004f98  0       10001cf8  10004f58  HDR+X    1000095   102    0
  5 active, 1000 total, 64 hash buckets
```

There are several important fields in this report, and some are rather cryptic.

- **address** is the internal address of the lock.

- **wtlist** is the address of the first user that is waiting for the lock. You can find the actual process id of the user by looking for the address in **tbstat -u**.

- **owner** is the address of the owner of the lock. To find the process id of the lock owner, look up the owner address in **tbstat -u**.

- **type** is the type of lock held. The type of lock is specified by the characters after the "+". The possible lock types are

    ```
    - X = Exclusive lock
    - IX = Intent exclusive lock
    - IS = Intent shared lock
    - S = Shared lock
    - U = Update lock
    ```

- **tblsnum** is the tblspace number (a unique identifier for the table). The first one or two digits are the dbspace number, as listed in **tbstat -d**, in which the table resides. The tblspace numbers ending in 02 are special database tablespaces used internally by the database server. To list the hexadecimal tblspace number for each table in a database, run the following SQL statement:

    ```
    select hex(partnum),tabname from systables
    ```

    Compare these values to the **tblsnum** column in **tbstat -d**.

- **rowid** identifies the actual item (row, table, or key) being locked. If the lock is on a table, the **rowid** is listed as 0. If the lock is on a page, the **rowid** ends in 00. For a key lock, the **rowid** will be listed as a large hexadecimal number; otherwise, the value is a **rowid** and the lock is on a row.

- **size** is used for a special type of lock on varchar columns, called a byte lock.

The **-u** option of **tbstat** shows a few things about locks, including the number of locks held and whether the user is waiting for a lock. Here is an example of **tbstat -u** output:

```
Users
address     flags     pid  user      tty    wait tout locks nreads nwrites
10001ba8    ------D   362  informix ttyp1  0    0    0     126    3
10001c18    ------D   0    informix ttyp1  0    0    0     0      0
10001c88    ------F   363  informix        0    0    0     0      0
10001cf8    --B----   387  george   ttyp1  0    0    5     6      11
```

If a user is waiting for a lock, the first column of the **flags** field would show "l", and the **wait** column would show the actual address of the lock, which you can trace back to the lock list in **tbstat -l**.

In the preceding example, user **george** has five locks. You can see what locks **george** has by looking for the address 10001cf8 in the **owner** column of **tbstat -k**.

Monitoring Lock Usage with INFORMIX-OnLine Dynamic Server

The administrator can get a good idea of how often a user must wait for another user to release a lock with the **onstat -p** command. The output of this command has a **lokwaits** column, which is incremented every time a user waits for a lock.

```
bufwaits lokwaits lockreqs deadlks dltouts ckpwaits compress seqscans
24708    40       8172128  0       0       2        80       161
```

In the preceding output, users had to wait for a lock to be released 40 times. You should monitor this value to see if it gets unusually high. If it does, you must monitor individual users and the number and type of locks they are holding.

Instead of using the **onstat** utility to monitor locks, consider using the SMI tables. SMI (System Monitoring Interface) is an SQL interface into the same memory structures that the **onstat** utility reads. To use SMI, select the **sysmaster** database from dbaccess. To list all users who own locks, run the following SQL statement:

```
select username,uid,waiter,dbsname,tabname,rowidlk,
   keynum,type
   from syslocks, syssessions
   where syssessions.sid = syslocks.owner
```

An example row from this output follows:

```
username     informix
uid          102
waiter
dbsname      bank1
tabname      transaction
rowidlk      0
keynum       0
type         X
```

The example shows a table lock on the **transaction** table. The **rowidlk** is listed as 0 if the lock is on a table. If any other session is waiting on the lock, the **session_id** is listed in the waiter column (however, only the first waiter is listed).

The lock type can be one of the following:

```
- X = Exclusive lock
- IX = Intent exclusive lock
- IS = Intent shared lock
- S = Shared lock
- U = Update lock
- SR = Shared repeatable read lock
```

You can also display the current locks in the system with **onstat -k**. A sample output follows. The descriptions for the columns in **syslocks** closely mirror the fields in the **onstat -k** output.

```
Locks
address   wtlist  owner   lklist  type    tblsnum  rowid  key#/bsiz
80f600    0       80a9d0  0       HDR+S   100002   205    0
80f628    0       80a9d0  80f600  HDR+X   100078   0      0
 2 active, 2000 total, 128 hash buckets
```

The fields in the lock output are explained next:

- **address** is the internal address of the lock.

- **wtlist** is the address of the first session that is waiting for the lock. You can find the actual session id of the user by looking for the address in **onstat -u**.

- **owner** is the address of the owner of the lock. To find the session id of the owner, look up the address in **onstat -u**.

- **type** is the type of lock held. The type of lock is specified by the characters after the "+". The possible lock types are

```
    - X = Exclusive lock
    - IX = Intent exclusive lock
    - IS = Intent shared lock
    - S = Shared lock
    - U = Update lock
    - SR = Shared repeatable read lock
```

- **tblsnum** is the tblspace number (a unique identifier for the table). The first one or two digits are the dbspace number, as listed in **onstat -d**, in which the table resides. The tblspace numbers ending in 02 are special database tablespaces used internally by the database server. To list the hexadecimal tblspace number for each table in a database, run the following SQL statement.

```
    select hex(partnum),tabname from systables
```

Compare these values to the tblsnum column in **onstat -d**.

- **rowid** is the actual row being locked. If the lock is on a table, the **rowid** is 0. If the lock is on a page, the **rowid** ends in 00. If the value is a key lock, the **rowid** is the rowid of the row itself.

- **key#** indicates that the lock is on a key. The key number starts with "k-".

- **size** is used for a special type of lock on varchar columns, called a byte lock.

The **-u** option of **onstat** shows a few things about locks, including the number of locks held and whether the user is waiting for a lock. Here is an example of **onstat -u** output:

```
Userthreads
address flags     sessid user        tty    wait     tout locks nreads nwrites
806cc8  ---P--D 0        informix   -      0        0    0     22     3
80702c  ---P--F 0        informix   -      0        0    0     0      0
807390  ---P--B 8        informix   -      0        0    0     0      0
8076f4  ---P--D 0        informix   -      0        0    0     0      0
80a9d0  Y--P--- 16       joe        ttyp0  adb044   0    2     0      0
80ad34  L--PR-- 18       ann        ttyp0  80f628   -1   1     0      0
 6 active, 20 total
```

If a user is waiting for a lock, the first column of the **flags** field shows an "L", and the **wait** column would show the actual address of the lock, which you can trace back to the lock list in **onstat -k**.

In the preceding example, user **joe** has one lock. You can see which lock **joe** has by looking for the address 80a9d0 in the **owner** column of **onstat -k**, shown earlier in this section. Also, the output shows **ann** waiting for a lock. From looking up the address of the lock for which **ann** is waiting in the **onstat -u** output (80f628), you can determine that **joe** owns the lock.

8.8   CASE STUDY (USING INFORMIX-ONLINE)

This case study uses sample output for INFORMIX-OnLine. However, the output would be very similar if INFORMIX-OnLine Dynamic Server was used.

Several users call you, the administrator, complaining that their "applications are hung." After ruling out the usual causes, such as full logs and a problem with the OnLine system (you can log in and access data with dbaccess), you decide to take a look at individual user activity with **tbstat -u**.

```
Users
address flags     pid user        tty    wait     tout   locks nreads nwrites
```

```
10001ba8 ------D 362 informix ttyp1 0        0      0      126    3
10001c18 ------D 0   informix ttyp1 0        0      0      0      0
10001c88 ------F 363 informix       0        0      0      0      0
10001cf8 --B---- 387 sandy    ttyp1 0        0      10384  21009  30438
10001d68 L---R-- 407 vijay    ttyp0 10004f58 -1     1      0      0
10001dd8 L---R-- 414 victor   ttyp3 10004f58 -1     1      0      0
```

You locate the users who have complained (**vijay** and **victor**) and notice from the flags field that they are both waiting for a lock. To find out who is holding the lock, you note the lock address in the wait column (10004f58) and find the entry with the same lock address in **tbstat -k**.

```
Locks
address    wtlist     owner      lklist     type    tblsnum   rowid  size
10004ed8   0          10001cf8   0          HDR+X   1000002   207    0
10004ef8   0          10001dd8   0          S       1000002   208    0
10004f18   0          10001cf8   10004f78   HDR+IX  1000095   0      0
10004f38   0          10001d68   0          S       1000002   208    0
10004f58   10001d68   10001cf8   10004f18   HDR+X   1000095   100    0
10004f78   0          10001cf8   10004ed8   HDR+S   1000002   208    0
```

Lock 10004f58 belongs to user 10001cf8. You look back in the first column of **tbstat -u** and find that user 10001cf8 is **sandy**. **Sandy** is in transaction (as indicated by the "B" in the second position of the flags column) and is currently holding 10,384 locks. This seems excessive, so you give Sandy a call and find out that she is running a batch update process. You make a note to talk to the systems analyst to see if the transaction can be run at night or broken up into smaller transactions.

You also notice something interesting about the lock for which Vijay and Victor are waiting. The **rowid** for the lock is 100. Since the rowid ends in 0, you know that the lock is on a page, not a specific row. This can seriously degrade concurrency and might be the reason several users are waiting. To find the table that has page-level locking, you look at the **tblsnum** column for the tablespace number, which is 1000095. You convert the number to decimal (16777365) and look up the table name in the **partnum** column of **systables**.

```
select tabname from systables where partnum = 16777365
```

You make a note to change the table to row-level locking tonight after the production users go home.

8.9   CHECKLIST FOR MONITORING LOCKS

Table 8.2 summarizes tuning issues for lock performance.

Table 8.2–Checklist for monitoring locks

What to Check	How to Check	How to Alter
Lock waits	**onstat -p** (lockwaits column)	Change locking strategy in applications
Is the lock table large enough?	**ovlock** field in **onstat -p**	LOCKS configuration parameter
Are applications using repeatable read?	Look for SET ISOLATION statements; ANSI databases use repeatable read as default	SET ISOLATION TO COMMITTED READ or SET ISOLATION TO CURSOR STABILITY
Do tables use row-level locking	select locklevel from systables where tabname = "*tabname*"	ALTER TABLE
Is dirty read used for reports or large queries using nonvolatile tables?	Look for SET ISOLATION statements	SET ISOLATION TO DIRTY READ
Can large update operations lock the table?		LOCK TABLE tabname IN EXCLUSIVE MODE
Are transactions as compact as possible?	Look for extraneous statements within transaction logic	Eliminate all unneeded code within a transaction

Chapter 9

Other Ways to Improve Performance

There are certain activities that may require a special configuration of the OnLine system. This chapter outlines the steps you can take to make these activities perform better. The activities discussed in this chapter are

- Data loads
- Indexing
- Batch delete programs
- Archiving
- High connection and network traffic load

9.1 DATA LOADS

Many applications require that a large amount of data be loaded into a table or set of tables, usually from an external source, such as a telephone switch or a mainframe database. Sometimes a load may occur only once when data are converted from a different file format into an INFORMIX database. Often the load program is run at off-peak hours and possibly has exclusive use of the tables. Some suggestions for improving performance in this kind of activity are listed here.

Increase the Checkpoint Interval

Checkpoints take precious time away from inserting data into a database. Since the data load will usually be INSERTing data into a small number of pages (unless the table has more than one index), the disk writes should be concentrated on a small number of pages.

If checkpoints normally occur every 10 minutes or less, consider increasing the checkpoint to 15 or 20 minutes for the data load. Unfortunately, to do this, you will have to increase CKPTINTVL and restart the OnLine system. Also, the physical log must be big enough to handle the before-image of pages written during the checkpoint interval.

Drop Indexes and Referential Constraints

A data load will proceed much faster without indexes on the table being loaded. If the data load is running when other users are not using the system and the number of rows being loaded is greater than approximately one-third of the number of rows in the table, dropping the indexes is advantageous. Also, if the table contains any constraints, these should be dropped before the load proceeds. Starting with version 7.10.UD1, you can disable constraints with the DISABLE command. In earlier versions, you must drop the constraint with an ALTER TABLE command.

Use INSERT Cursors

INSERT cursors are a fast method of putting data in a table. INSERT cursors buffer rows in the front end before sending them to the database server to process. You can get significantly better performance by using INSERT cursors to load data rather than an INSERT statement because of the decrease in the amount of messages that must be passed between the application and database server.

The only difficulty of using INSERT cursors is that if a failure occurs for some reason, it is difficult to determine which row caused the failure. The added error checking requires some extra coding in the application.

PREPARE Statements That Are Used Repeatedly

If you are unable to use an INSERT cursor because of error-checking difficulties, the INSERT statement should be PREPAREd first and EXECUTEd repeatedly. The PREPARE statement parses the SQL statement once and cuts down on the amount of message passing and the work done by the database server when the statement is executed many times.

Use LOAD Instead of the dbload Utility

The LOAD command is more efficient than the **dbload** utility for loading formatted data from a sequential file. Unfortunately, the LOAD command is very simple and lacks some of the features available with dbload. For the best performance use LOAD, or, if you need a more controlled environment, use INSERT cursors.

9.2 INDEXING

Index creation (see Fig. 9.1) is an operation all administrators wish ran faster because the table is locked and unavailable during the index build. INFORMIX-OnLine Dynamic Server has a parallel index build feature that allows indexes to be built even faster than in INFORMIX-OnLine.

An index build consists of the following activities:

- The data are read from disk into the buffer pool, unless they are already cached in the buffer pool.
- The key is extracted and sorted. The preliminary sort dramatically improves the performance of the index build because the b-tree pages can be filled sequentially. The sort uses memory for smaller tables. For larger tables, both memory and disk are used to sort the keys.
- The b-tree is built with the sorted keys. In INFORMIX-OnLine Dynamic Server, larger indexes will be built in parallel, with each thread building a part of the subtree which is finally put together into one b-tree.

Figure 9.1-How an index is created

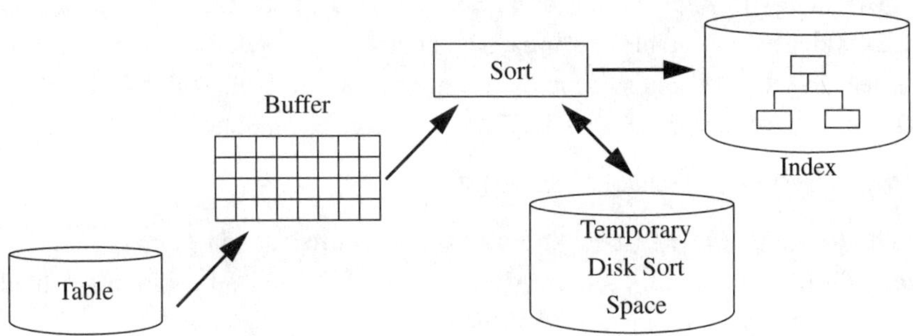

There are a few things you can do to improve performance of index builds.

Perform Parallel Sorts

The sort routine itself takes up a good percentage of the time needed to create the index. To speed up the sort, you can use the parallel sort routine. Parallel sorting is activated by setting the PSORT_NPROCS environment variable to the number of processes (or threads in INFORMIX-OnLine Dynamic Server) that will perform the sort. The environment variable should be set before starting the application process that runs the CREATE INDEX statement.

Although parallel sorting shows the most performance gain with a multiprocessor system, a single-processor system may benefit from PSORT_NPROCS set to 2. Even though there is only one processor to perform the work, one sort routine may be waiting for a disk read or write, while the other may be using the processor.

Spread Sort Files Across Disks

Sorting large tables will usually mean that the sort routine cannot do all its work in memory, and temporary sort runs must be written to disk. To decrease disk contention, spread the temporary sort files across disks.

In INFORMIX-OnLine, temporary sort files are written to one or more file system directories. If you are running a parallel sort, you can set the environment variable PSORT_DBTEMP to multiple directories.

```
PSORT_NPROCS = /sortdir1:/sortdir2
```

The first sort file will be created in **/sortdir1**, the second in **/sortdir2**, the third in **/sortdir1**, and so on. Obviously, these two directories should be in file systems on different disks.

In INFORMIX-OnLine Dynamic Server, you can send temporary sort files to dbspaces, which are preferable to using UNIX directories because the chunks are usually a raw device. To set the location of multiple sort files, use either the DBSPACETEMP configuration parameter or the DBSPACETEMP environment variable.

```
DBSPACETEMP = dbtemp1,dbtemp2
```

The first sort file will be created in the **dbtemp1** dbspace, the second in the **dbtemp2** dbspace, the third in **dbtemp1**, and so on. The chunks for **dbtemp1** should be on a different disk than the chunks for **dbtemp2**.

Increase Read-Ahead Parameters (INFORMIX-OnLine Dynamic Server)

The read-ahead parameters in the INFORMIX-OnLine Dynamic Server allow the I/O subsystem (either the AIO vps or kernel AIO) to attempt to read pages from disk into the shared memory buffer pool before they are needed by the session. Since an index build must read every page in the table, it is an excellent candidate to take advantage of read-ahead. You may consider increasing RA_PAGES to make sure that enough pages are read into shared memory to keep up with the index build process.

9.3   LARGE DELETE OPERATIONS

Another operation that causes great upheaval in an OnLine system is one that removes a large number of rows from one or more tables. Sometimes a DELETE operation is combined with an operation that moves these rows to an archive or history table.

Here are some recommendations for improving performance for a large DELETE operation.

Drop Indexes First

When a row is deleted, the database server must find the key in each index and delete it as well as the actual row itself. In large indexes with three or four levels, this might mean a few extra disk reads for each index. Depending on the number of rows you are deleting, it may be faster to drop indexes first, before deleting a large number of rows.

Another reason to drop indexes first is that a massive delete operation may leave the existing index very sparsely populated, hurting performance on subsequent operations that use the index. You can see the average number of free bytes per index node of an index by running the following command:

```
oncheck -pT database:table
```

If the b-tree pages are less than half full on average, you will substantially decrease the size of the index by rebuilding.

Since the table is locked while the index is being created, dropping indexes before a DELETE operation may not be feasible for databases used 24 hours a day.

Lock the Table in Exclusive Mode

If the delete operation is using the table exclusively, lock the table before deleting rows.

```
LOCK TABLE tabname IN EXCLUSIVE MODE
```

Locking the table decreases the amount of locking operations that must occur for each DELETE statement. It also decreases the chance that you will run out of OnLine locks during the delete operation. Finally, in INFORMIX-OnLine Dynamic Server, locking the table decreases the overhead of marking the row for DELETE and directing the b-tree-cleaner thread to DELETE the row when the transaction is committed.

Avoid a Long Transaction

A *long transaction* is a transaction that starts in the first log and spans a percentage of the logs given by the LTXHWM configuration parameter. A long transaction will be rolled back by the database server.

If your application deletes a large number of rows in one transaction, you should make sure there is enough log space to hold the transaction. One entry is placed in the logical log for every row deleted and for every index key deleted. To make a rough estimation of the amount of space used by a DELETE transaction, run a DELETE statement that deletes only a small number of rows. Then you can examine the logs to see how much log space was used with **tbstat -l** or **onstat -l**, or run the **tblog** utility to see the size of each log entry:

1. Run the following command (note that the resulting file may be very large) to dump the log files on disk:

    ```
    tblog >tblog.out
    ```

2. Examine the **tblog.out** file with an editor. Look for DELITEM (index key delete) and HDELETE (row delete) transaction types. The **len** field will give you an idea of how long each transaction record is. A sample entry follows:

    ```
    addr   len   type      xid   id   link
    18     40    DELITEM   5     1    1f37c4 100039 3915 199 3 4
    ```

Guarding against long transactions is not exactly providing a performance improvement. However, the consequences of a long transaction do have an impact performance. If a long transaction occurs, it is rolled back, which takes almost as much time as performing the transaction itself.

9.4   IMPROVING ARCHIVE PERFORMANCE

An archive is a necessary part of the daily activity of a system, but it has a negative impact on the performance of other processing that is occurring at the same time, especially for an OnLine system running 24 hours a day. Normally, an archive should be planned for the time of day when there is the least amount of activity in the OnLine system.

Here are some suggestions for improving the performance of an archive.

Invest in a Fast Tape Drive

For INFORMIX-OnLine systems, this is the best advice for improving overall performance, since multiple tape drives cannot be used.

OnLine allows archives to remote-tape devices. However, the extra network operations required to transfer data across the network will impact archive performance.

Use Parallel Archiving (INFORMIX-OnLine Dynamic Server)

The ON-Archive utility can archive dbspaces in parallel (see Fig. 9.2). This means that if you have multiple tape drives, they can be used to archive the OnLine system in parallel. One or more dbspaces can be assigned to a particular dbspace set, which then can be archived to a specific tape drive.

Figure 9.2-Parallel archiving

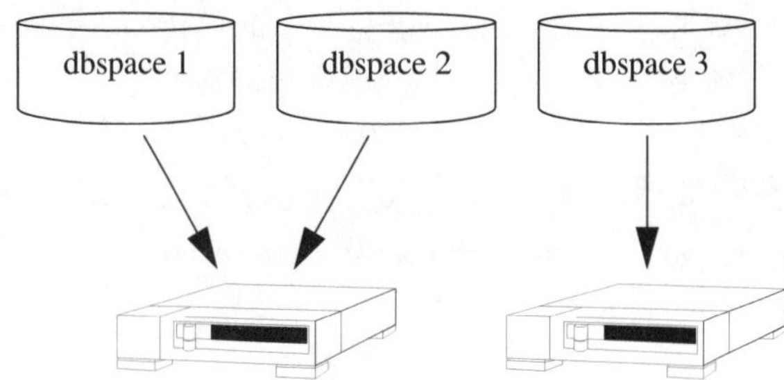

Parallel archiving will be most efficient when the tables can be spread evenly between the tape drives. Keep this in mind when planning locations of tables and dbspaces.

Archive Only Active Tables Nightly (INFORMIX-OnLine Dynamic Server)

The ON-Archive utility allows you to archive only specific dbspaces. This feature gives you extensive freedom in planning nightly backups. Consider archiving the most used tables nightly and static tables less often. However, a restore may take longer with this method, because the restore must cycle through all the log tapes looking for transactions for that table, even though there may be none.

Move Very Large Tables to Another OnLine System (INFORMIX-OnLine)

In INFORMIX-OnLine, you do not have very many options for archiving very large databases, because the entire OnLine system must be archived at once. Also, it is important to consider the time to complete a restore process on a large database.

One way to cut down on archive and restore time is to move very large tables to another OnLine system. The OnLine system can be on the same machine as the first OnLine system or a remote machine. Since each OnLine system has its own archive and restore processes, you can restore or archive both OnLine systems in parallel. This strategy works best with tables that are not used often, such as history tables, because of the added overhead of accessing a table in another OnLine system.

9.5   CONFIGURING THE ONLINE SYSTEM FOR A LARGE NUMBER OF CONNECTIONS

An OnLine system with a large number of user connections will have its own performance bottlenecks that the administrator should plan to avoid. Usually, when there is a large number of connections, the application processes will reside on one or more client systems, different from the system the database server resides on. This configuration is most common because most UNIX systems simply cannot handle a database server and a large number of application processes simultaneously.

Here are some suggestions on how to achieve the best performance in a heavily used client/server environment.

Guard Against Network Overload

One or more network packets will be sent to the database server every time the application processes an SQL statement. The database server sends one or more network packets when data must be returned to the application or an SQL statement has completed execution. And of course, when an application connects to the database server, a message must be sent to initiate the connection request.

All these messages can add up to a network overload when hundreds or even thousands of users are connected. If a network is overloaded, the number of packet collisions (where multiple users try to send a packet over the network at one time) increase. You can see the number of packet collisions in your system by running the UNIX **netstat** utility. The following example shows the network packets and collisions every 2 seconds, with the first line showing statistics since the system was last rebooted.

```
netstat -i 2
 input (lo0)   output               input     (Total)     output
packets errs  packets errs  colls  packets errs  packets  errs colls
83391   0     83391   0     200    83391   0     83395    2    23
229     0     229     0     0      229     0     229      0    0
68      0     68      0     0      68      0     68       0    0
66      0     66      0     0      66      0     66       0    0
```

This example shows very few collisions for the number of packets that have been sent and received.

If your network is overloaded, consider breaking the network into subnetworks. In INFORMIX-OnLine Dynamic Server, you can divide connections up into multiple network interface cards. To do this, you need two entries in the **/etc/hosts** file, two entries in the **$INFORMIXDIR/etc/sqlhosts** file, and two entries in the **/etc/services** file.

The **$INFORMIXDIR/etc/sqlhosts** file might look something like this:

```
interface1    onsoctcp    hostname1    soc1
interface2    onsoctcp    hostname2    soc2
```

The **/etc/hosts** file will have two entries, one for each network interface card.

```
192.133.104.19    hostname1
192.133.104.20    hostname2
```

The application will connect using one of the interface cards; you specify which with the INFORMIXSERVER environment variable. This example shows how to set the environment variable using the Bourne shell:

```
INFORMIXSERVER=interface1
export INFORMIXSERVER
```

Finally, you must have both server names, **interface1** and **interface2**, in the OnLine configuration file.

```
DBSERVERNAME    interface1
DBSERVERALIAS   interface2
```

Starting with version 7.10.UD1, you use an asterisk (*) in the host name field of the **sqlhosts** file to signify multiple ethernet cards:

```
server    ontlitcp    *    1284
```

The server uses a TCP system call to find all possible IP addresses to listen to.

Decrease the Message Traffic if the Network Is Slow

If network traffic is a problem or if the client and server are separated by a slow wide-area network, make sure the number of network messages is kept to a minimum.

- PREPARE statements that are reused whenever possible. The PREPARE statement performs the initial parse of the SQL statement. Once a statement is prepared, the subsequent execution does not have to perform the parse operation again, cutting down on the number of messages passed back and forth between the application and the database server.

- Use stored procedures for activities that execute more than three SQL statements without passing messages back to the application. Although stored procedures have their own overhead, they are most efficient when there are multiple SQL statements that must be executed together. If these statements do not pass messages back to the user, they are even more efficient when executed in a stored procedure.

- Don't return rows or columns unless they are needed by the application. Sometimes novice programmers retrieve more data with an SQL statement than is needed and eliminate unneeded data in the application. This is a poor programming practice, especially when the network can be a bottleneck.

Increase the Number of Poll Threads (INFORMIX-OnLine Dynamic Server)

INFORMIX-OnLine Dynamic Server receives messages from the client application through a specific thread called the poll thread. If many applications are trying to send messages at the same time, the poll thread may not be able to keep up. For more than 50 active users connecting through TCP/IP, you may benefit through an increase in the number of poll threads. Shared memory connections use a poll thread as well, but the shared memory poll thread has much less work to do than the TCP/IP poll thread and can handle more users.

The NETTYPE configuration parameter specifies, among other things, the number of poll threads that will be started. The number of poll threads is specified in the second field in the NETTYPE parameter. The following example shows two poll threads configured for the TCP/IP TLI protocol.

```
NETTYPE TLITCP,2,100,CPU
```

Another important field in NETTYPE specifies the vp on which the poll thread(s) run. The fourth field can specify either CPU, for the CPU vp, or NET, for the network vp. You should place the poll threads for the most important protocol used in your system on the CPU vp. Only one poll thread can run on a single vp. If users communicate through either shared memory or TCP/IP, the poll thread from one protocol should run on the CPU vp, while the poll thread for the other protocol runs on the network vp; for example,

```
NETTYPE TLITCP,2,100,CPU
NETTYPE IPCSHM,1,50,NET
```

Since only one poll thread can run on a vp, this configuration requires that two CPU vps be running; otherwise, only one poll thread will be started. Set the number of CPU vps with the NUMCPUVPS configuration parameter.

Chapter 10

Fragmentation and Parallel Database Query

Versions of INFORMIX-OnLine Dynamic Server starting with 7.0 have two features key to performance: Parallel Database Query (PDQ) and Fragmentation. Both features promise to improve performance in some OnLine activities, most notably in decision support queries. This chapter discusses the two features and how they can be utilized to improve performance. Some of the topics covered follow:

- What is fragmentation?
- Strategies for fragmentation
- What is Parallel Database Query?
- Parallel inserts
- How to monitor and tune PDQ

10.1 WHAT IS FRAGMENTATION?

Fragmentation is a method of intelligently spreading a table across disks to improve performance. Although earlier versions of OnLine had a method of striping a table across disks by adding multiple chunks from different disks to the same dbspace, you could not easily control how the data were sent to each chunk.

Some of the advantages of fragmentation follow:

- Fragmentation is a key component of Parallel Data Query, allowing OnLine to scan each fragment in parallel to read large amounts of data quickly.
- Some queries or other SQL operations may need to search only one fragment on one disk, rather than through the entire table.
- If many users are executing operations on a fragmented table concurrently, a table spread across many disks may cut down on disk contention between users.

How a Table Is Fragmented

Each fragment resides on a different dbspace. To fragment a table across disks, chunks for each dbspace should reside on different disks. When you create a fragmented table, you specify which part of the table will reside on each dbspace (see Fig. 10.1).

Figure 10.1-A fragmented table

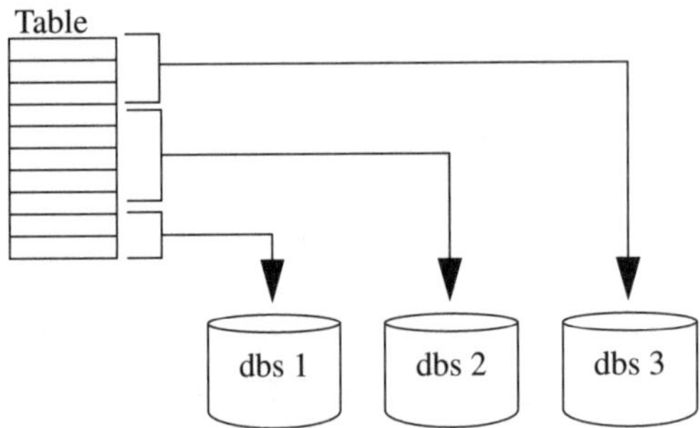

There are two methods of fragmenting a table:

- **Round robin.** This method randomly places rows on one of the fragments for a table. An example of a table created with round-robin fragmentation on two fragments follows:

```
create table customer(
        customer_num       serial
        customer_lname     char(20))
        fragment by round robin in dbs1,dbs2;
```

- **Expression-based.** This method places rows on a fragment based on an expression. For example, you may want to place all rows where **employee_lname** are between A and L in one fragment, and all rows where **employee_lname** are between M and Z in another fragment. An example of a table created with expression-based fragmentation follows:

```
    create table customer(
        customer_num       serial
        customer_lname     char(20))
        fragment by expression
            customer_lname       >= "A",
            customer_lname       <= "L" in dbs1,
            customer_lname       >  "L" in dbs2;
```

Each fragment is put in its own set of extents with its own table space number.

You can also fragment an index. By default, an index of a fragmented table is fragmented in the same way as the table. You can also create an index with its own fragmentation scheme.

```
create index idx1 on customer(customer_num)
      fragment by expression
      customer_num < 100000 in dbs1,
      customer_num >= 100000   in dbs2;
```

When an index is fragmented, each fragment is put in its own set of extents with its own table space number. This means that the index pages are not intermingled with data pages, as they are in unfragmented tables.

The disk layout for the example fragmentation of the customer table is shown in Figure 10.2.

Figure 10.2-Sample fragmentation diagram

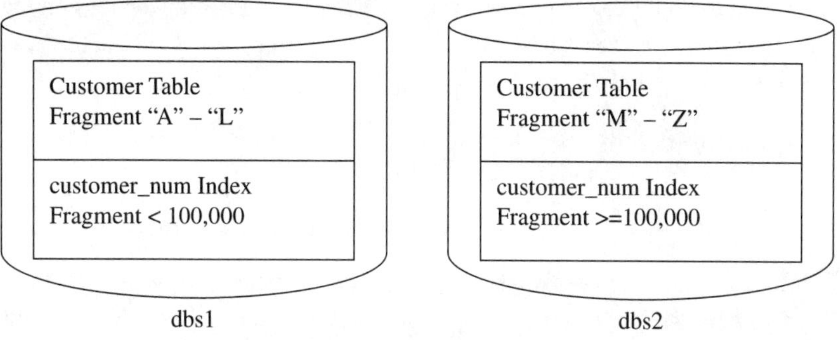

You can think of an index fragment as its own separate b-tree. A session may be able to read only one index fragment to retrieve data. In the fragmentation example shown in Figure 10.2, a SELECT statement with a WHERE clause such as "WHERE customer_num = 200000" would read only the b-tree in dbs2. The b-tree in fragment in dbs1 is not examined. If another session simultaneously executes a SELECT statement with a WHERE clause such as "WHERE customer_num = 20000", this session will read only the b-tree in the fragment in dbs1. Performance will probably improve because each session is reading a separate disk. Without a fragmented index, the sessions would be competing for I/O against the same disk.

An index can be moved to a different dbspace than the data without being fragmented. This strategy is preferred for smaller tables or tables that are not used frequently.

```
create index idx1 on customer(customer_num)
       in dbs2;
```

How OnLine Uses a Fragmented Table and Index

Suppose that the **customer** table is fragmented by **customer_lname** and its index is fragmented by **customer_num**, as shown in the previous example. A decision support query executed on this table might be:

```
select * from customer group by customer_num
```

In this example, all fragments must be scanned, since **customer_lname** is not included as a filter in the query. For a decision support query (a query that will read a large amount of data), one thread will be assigned to scan each fragment.

Consider the following query:

```
select * from customer where customer_lname > "N"
```

In this example, the optimizer can determine from the fragmentation expression that only the second fragment must be read, so only one thread will be started to scan that fragment. The other fragments will not be read.

What happens if a decision support query can use an index, such as the following query?

```
select * from customer where customer_num > 120000
```

In this case, since the **customer_num** index is fragmented by **customer_num**, only one index fragment will be read to find the location of the data. The best scenario would be if the index fragment read is significantly smaller than the entire index would be if it was not fragmented.

10.2 FRAGMENTATION STRATEGIES

The following suggestions are for achieving the best performance by fragmenting a table and its indexes.

- Fragment to spread I/O across disks. The decision support query will start a scan thread for each fragment it must read. The scan threads should have an equal amount of work to do.

- Don't overfragment. Each fragment for a table should reside on a separate disk. There is some overhead to opening a fragment to scan, so don't create very small fragments. Also, don't bother fragmenting tables and indexes that aren't used often.

- Keep fragmentation expressions simple. Overly complicated expressions might confuse the optimizer, which must determine what fragments should be read for a query. The SET EXPLAIN output shows which fragments will be read. You should plan to test your fragmentation scheme against production queries using a test database first. The following is a sample output of SET EXPLAIN, which shows that all fragments will be scanned for the query.

```
QUERY:
------
select number from account order by number

Estimated Cost: 2
Estimated # of Rows Returned: 10
Temporary Files Required For: Order By

1)informix.account: SEQUENTIAL SCAN(Parallel, fragments: ALL)
```

- Generally, fragment indexes by their key values. Queries that can use only one or two index fragments will benefit by the smaller number of index pages. Fragmenting indexes increases concurrency because different users may be reading different fragments at one time.

- Don't fragment tables on columns whose values change frequently. If the column is updated, the row or key value might need to be moved from one fragment to another, resulting in some processing overhead. Also, fragmentation on date columns or any other rapidly increasing column may cause the administrator to constantly rearrange the fragmentation scheme.

- Choose round-robin fragmentation when the table is usually read sequentially (usually in queries without a WHERE clause) or when there is no column that can be used to evenly spread data across disks.

- There is a small amount of overhead in evaluating an expression. When inserting a large number of rows into table fragmented by expression, you may see some degradation in performance. If INSERT/UPDATE/DELETE speed is critical, round-robin fragmentation is best.

- Don't index columns unless they are used for OLTP queries. In earlier versions of OnLine, a query executed very slowly if it could not use an index. With the advent of hash joins (a new method of joining tables) and parallel scans, it might be much faster for the database server to scan the data sequentially rather than use the index. Although the optimizer should make this determination, it cannot always do so.

Note that there are other considerations in fragmenting tables and indexes, such as archiving, fault tolerance, and administration. These issues are not covered in this book but should be analyzed by the administrator before embarking on a fragmentation strategy.

10.3 CASE STUDY

To illustrate fragmentation guidelines, here is an example of how a table might be fragmented. The table is called **transaction** and holds all transactions for an account.

```
create table transaction(
        trans_id        serial,
        trans_amt       money(12,2),
        trans_date      date,
        trans_type      char(2),
        account_nbr     integer);

create index idx1 on transaction(account_nbr);
create index idx2 on transaction(trans_date);
```

Before deciding on a fragmentation strategy, examine how the data are used. The most methodical way to do this is to examine key applications and extract the queries. You determine the most important queries and how often they are executed. You pinpoint one very important decision support query that is used to produce a nightly transaction report.

```
select * from account, transaction
   where account.account_nbr = transaction.account_nbr
      group by trans_type
```

You also examine and pinpoint the most important OLTP query; that is, a query that examines only a few rows. Usually, OLTP queries must be completed quickly. The crucial OLTP query you identify is

```
select * from account, transaction
   where account.account_nbr = transaction.account_nbr
   and account_nbr = ?
```

Probably the best table fragmentation scheme would be one that would spread the decision support query across multiple disks. There may be a few columns that can be used to fragment data, but the administrator determines that the **trans_type** (transaction type) column might produce a good spread.

The best index fragmentation scheme for **idx1** is on **account_nbr**, since a query on the index must read only one fragment. Even though **account_nbr** is a serial field in another table (**account**), you determine that account numbers do not get assigned very quickly, and a fragmentation scheme on this value may be fairly stable.

It might not be a good idea to fragment the **idx2** index at all. The **trans_date** column is not a good candidate because date columns tend to increase constantly, causing the administrator to create new fragments for the newer dates and deleting fragments with older dates. Instead, you decide to put the index in a separate dbspace.

The schema for our newly fragmented table might look something like this:

```
create table transaction(
        trans_id         serial,
        trans_amt        money(12,2),
        trans_date       date,
        trans_type       char(2),
        account_nbr      integer)
    fragment by expression
        trans_type = "d" or trans_type = "c" in dbs1,
        trans_type = "e" or trans_type = "m" in dbs2,
        remainder in dbs3;

create index idx1 on transaction(account_nbr)
    fragment by expression
        account_nbr < 100000 in dbs4,
        account_nbr >= 100000 and account_nbr < 200000 in dbs5,
        account_nbr >= 200000 in dbs6;
create index idx2 on transaction(trans_date) in dbs6;
```

10.4 PARALLEL DATABASE QUERY

Another very important feature to performance in an OnLine system is Parallel Database Query. PDQ is a method to parallelize a *decision support query*, or a query that must work with many rows in one or more tables. PDQ is effective on multiprocessor systems with multiple disks.

The database server divides a decision support query into multiple pieces and gives each piece to a separate thread. One scan thread will be started for each fragment in the table to be queried. Join threads perform joins between two tables. Group threads perform any sorting required by ORDER BY or GROUP BY statements. In most cases, the threads can do their work in parallel. For example, two scan threads that scan data from disk can work in parallel.

All the threads performing a query run on the CPU virtual processor. Since all CPU vps share the same ready queue, this means that the threads may or may not be running at once. The true degree of parallelism also depends on the other activity in the OnLine system, since there are other operations running in an OnLine system and sharing the CPU vp.

Figure 10.3 shows that the relationship between threads and virtual processors is variable. It shows that two threads are running in parallel, one that scans data and one that joins the data from one table to another. Several other threads are involved in the query (another scan thread and a join thread) waiting for a CPU vp to become free so that they can run. Other users' threads can also be in the ready queue or running on a CPU vp. The

Figure 10.3-Parallel Data Query—threads, vps, and processors

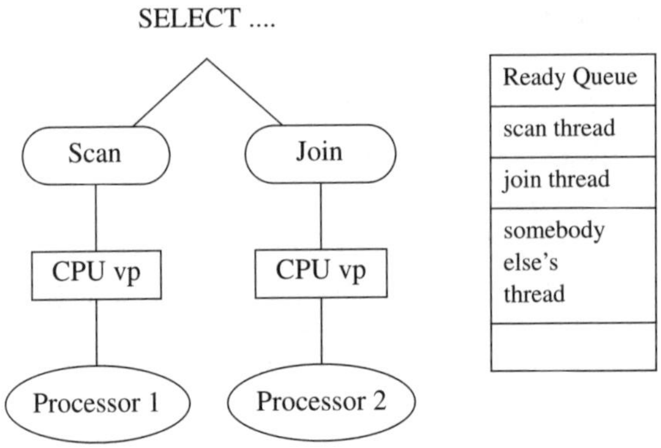

SELECT ....

Scan   Join

CPU vp   CPU vp

Processor 1   Processor 2

Ready Queue

scan thread

join thread

somebody else's thread

relationship between virtual processors and hardware processors in a system may also be variable, depending on the other work that is occurring in the system. In Figure 10.3, the two CPU vps are running on two separate processors. However, at any time, the processes may be replaced by other processes in the system needing to perform work.

Another key feature of parallel query is that the buffer pool will sometimes be bypassed (automatically by the database server) when large amounts of data must be read for the query. This feature is called *light scans* and can be monitored by **onstat -g lsc**. Since updating pages in the buffer pool can be time-consuming, light scans can really improve performance for decision support queries.

10.5 PARALLEL INSERTS

Starting with version 7.10.UD1, OnLine also runs certain inserts in parallel.

- INSERT INTO ... SELECT FROM statements will be parallelized in two ways. First the SELECT part of the statement will be parallelized as any other SELECT statement. The INSERT will also be parallelized if the target table is fragmented.
- SELECT ... INTO TEMP statements are also parallelized in two ways. The SELECT segment is parallelized as is the INSERT into the temporary table. The temporary table will automatically be fragmented by the database server, based on the number of dbspaces specified by DBSPACETEMP.

The parallel insert is performed by insert threads. These threads read data passed from the scan threads that read data from the SELECT segment of the statement. Neither the scan threads nor the insert threads perform the database I/O. They simply place requests in the AIO queue for the kernel AIO mechanism or for the AIO vps.

10.6 HOW TO MONITOR AND TUNE PDQ

Left unchecked, a decision support query could spawn 10 or 20 threads that would use all the available resources on the system. Imagine what multiple decision support queries could do to a system!

Although the fastest way to perform a query is to give the query all the resources it could possibly use, other work may need to be completed during the same time frame. The administrator has the ability to determine how much *resource*, meaning memory, disk, and CPU (through the number of threads), can be used to perform a query. Once the administrator specifies the amount of resource a query can have, it is up to a part of the database server called the *Memory Grant Manager* (MGM) to determine whether a query can proceed with the amount of resources it has requested. If the MGM determines the query cannot proceed, it will wait in a queue until enough resource has been freed by other running queries.

Configuration Parameters

The configuration parameters that control PDQ are listed next:

- **PDQPRIORITY.** The PDQPRIORITY configuration parameter sets the amount of resources that will be used by an individual query. If PDQPRIORITY is set to 0, no parallelism is used—the query runs as it would with earlier versions. If PDQPRIOR-ITY is set to 1, scan threads are started in parallel (one per disk involved in the fragment), but no other parallelism is used in the query. If PDQPRIORITY is set from 2 to 100, some parallelism beyond multiple scan threads is used. In this case, you can think of PDQPRIORITY as a percentage of the total amount of resource the query uses in comparison to how much it would receive if it could get as much as it wanted. For example, if PDQPRIORITY is set to 50, a query would run with 50% of the number of threads and memory it would use at 100%. PDQPRIORITY can also be used as an environment variable for a particular application's session, or in a program (with the SET PDQPRIORITY statement) to override the configuration parameter.

- **MAX_PDQPRIORITY.** Since PDQPRIORITY can be set by an application developer or a user, MAX_PDQPRIORITY allows the administrator to make sure that users do not request 100% of available resource. The PDQPRIORITY is multiplied by (MAX_PDQPRIORITY/100) to obtain the actual priority that is used. For example, if PDQPRIORITY is set by a session at 100 and MAX_PDQPRIORITY is set to 50, then the true priority used for the query is 100 * (50/100) = 50.

- **DS_TOTAL_MEMORY.** The administrator can also cap the amount of shared memory used for decision support queries with the DS_TOTAL_MEMORY configuration parameter. DS_TOTAL_MEMORY is a subset of the shared memory that is allocated to the entire OnLine system. It is allocated from the virtual shared memory for the OnLine system.

- **DS_MAX_QUERIES.** The DS_MAX_QUERIES parameter specifies the number of decision support queries that can run at once. If DS_MAX_QUERIES is set to 5, only five queries that are classified as decision support queries can run at once. All other queries must wait until a running query completes. All nondecision support queries can run at any time.

The PDQ parameters can also be set dynamically with the *onmode utility.*

These parameters give the administrator a great deal of flexibility; however, they can be difficult to tune. For example, the administrator may need to decide if it is better to let five decision support queries run at once or to let only three run at once and let the other two wait.

Classification of Decision Support Queries

The optimizer does not classify which queries are decision support queries and which are OLTP queries. Instead, it makes this classification by the value of PDQPRIOR-ITY. If PDQPRIORITY is 0, the query is OLTP and will not pass through the Memory Grant Manager. If PDQPRIORITY is higher than 0, the query will pass through the Memory Grant Manger. OLTP queries will usually suffer if passed through the MGM, primarily if they have to wait to run.

If an application runs both OLTP and decision support queries, the programmer will have to embed SET PDQPRIORITY statements within the program (if using pre 7.0 applications, PREPARE the SET PDQPRIORITY statement). This method makes it difficult for the administrator to tune the query's resource usage. It is best to first tune the query outside of the application to determine the appropriate value of PDQPRIORITY.

Monitoring the Memory Grant Manager

The **onstat -g mgm** command shows the status of decision support queries—how many are waiting, how much resource each query is using, and so on. This output and some query timings are the principal method an administrator has for tuning the PDQ parameters. It will also be used to determine why a query might be waiting to run.

Here's a sample **onstat -g mgm** report, with explanations of each section interspersed.

```
Memory Grant Manager (MGM)
--------------------------
```

This section lists the current setting of the memory grant manager configuration parameters.

```
MAX_PDQ_PRIORITY: 100
DS_MAX_QUERIES: 3
DS_MAX_SCANS: 10
DS_TOTAL_MEMORY: 3000 KB
```

This section lists the number of active queries, the number of ready queries (queries that are waiting for a resource to run, e.g., memory, scan threads, DS_MAX_QUERIES), and the total number of decision support queries that can run at one time (DS_MAX_QUERIES).

```
Queries:   Active   Ready   Maximum
             3         0       3
```

This section lists the total amount of memory available for decision support queries (DS_TOTAL_MEMORY) and the amount of free memory. Memory is allocated to a query in units of a quantum, which is DS_TOTAL_MEMORY/DS_MAX_QUERIES; in the example, this is 3000/3 = 1000. This value is listed in the **Quantum** column. This means that 1000 kbytes will be reserved for a query even if it is not used.

```
Memory:   Total   Free   Quantum
(KB)      3000     0     1000
```

This section lists the total number of scan threads available for decision support queries (DS_MAX_SCANS) and the number of scan threads available. Scan threads are allocated in units of a quantum, which is DS_MAX_SCANS/DS_MAX_QUERIES, which is 10/3 = 3 (rounded down). The **Quantum** column lists this size. Scan threads are allocated in units of a quantum, even though the quantum may not be used by one query.

```
Scans:    Total   Free   Quantum
           10       7       3
```

This section lists the number of decision support queries that are waiting for a particular resource. The query must be granted all the necessary resources before it can run. If a user complains that a query is "hanging," the administrator should examine the output of **onstat -g mgm** first, before assuming that there is a problem within the server. Each resource can be thought of as a "gate": the gate cannot be entered until enough resources are available. Each "gate" the query can wait on is listed next, with the number of queries waiting for that resource.

```
Load Control: (Memory)  (Scans)  (Priority)  (Max Queries)  (Reinit)
              Gate 1    Gate 2   Gate 3      Gate 4         Gate 5
(Queue Length) 0          0        0           0              0
```

The next section lists the active decision support queries. Two numbers are listed in the **Memory** and **Thread** columns: the number of scan threads currently used/granted and the amount of memory currently being used/granted. The memory is in units of 8 kbytes. The following example shows each query using 1000 kbytes of memory. Only the third query is currently scanning the table.

```
Active Queries:
----------------

Session    Query     Priority    Thread    Memory     Scans    Gate
10         c666c0    2           be62d8    125/125    0/1      -
12         c726c0    2           bfa508    125/125    0/1      -
11         c6c6c0    2                     125/125    1/1      -
```

This section lists any decision support queries waiting on a resource and the resource they are waiting on. The following example shows no query waiting.

```
Ready Queries: None
```

Finally, the last section shows an average of the amount of memory and scan threads that were free, as well as the average number of queries that were active at once and in the ready queue.

```
Free Resource     Average #         Minimum #
---------------   ---------------   ---------

Memory            93.8 +- 119.7     0
Scans             7.5 +- 1.3        6
Queries           Average   #       Maximum #    Total #
---------------   ---------------   ---------    -------

Active            2.3 +- 1.0        3            4
Ready             1.0 +- 0.0        1            1
```

Granted Memory Versus Allocated Memory

The Memory Grant Manager reserves or grants only a percentage of memory. The amount of memory actually used by the query may be equal to or less than the amount of memory granted. You can determine how much memory a query needs by setting PDQ-PRIORITY to 100 and running the query. While the query is running, monitor the shared memory pools with **onstat -g mem**. An example of **onstat -g mem** follows:

```
Blkpool summary
name    class    addr          size      #blks
3       V        c115534a8     507904    62
3       V        c115534e0     573440    70
```

To determine how much memory is allocated, add up the values in the **#blks** column for the session and multiply by 8 kbytes. In the preceding example, session 3 has two pools: the first is 62 * 8 = 496 kbytes and 70 * 8 = 560 kbytes.

If the amount of memory allocated as shown in **onstat -g mem** is less than the amount of memory granted, you can safely reduce PDQPRIORITY for the query without reducing the amount of memory given to the query. In a finely tuned system, no query will run with PDQPRIORITY higher than needed to acquire the maximum amount of memory.

Unfortunately, there are other factors that affect the query performance—CPU (# threads) and disk I/O (# scan threads). These factors are also determined by the value of PDQPRIORITY. By reducing PDQPRIORITY to match the allocated memory to the reserved memory, you may also be reducing the number of scan threads and intermediate threads allocated to perform the query. The only way to determine how this affects query performance is to time the query with different PDQPRIORITY values.

10.7 CASE STUDY

You have been receiving sporadic complaints about large queries that are running slowly. One user states that a query can run in 10 minutes early in the morning but runs in 30 minutes during peak hours.

The large disparity in response time at different hours leads you to wonder if the queries are waiting for some reason. You run **onstat -g mgm** and receive the following output:

```
Load Control   (Memory) (Scans)    (Priority)(Max Queries)  (Reinit)
               Gate 1   Gate 2     Gate 3    Gate 4         Gate 5
(Queue Length) 0        0          2         0              0

Active Queries
--------------

Session    Query        Priority    Thread      Memory    Scans    Gate
17         a36b878      100                     28/32     2/2      -
Ready Queries
--------------

Session    Query        Priority    Thread      Memory    Scans    Gate
14         a37b878      100         a5bdb60     0/32      0/2      3
15         a383878      100         a5ac0b0     0/32      0/2      3
```

After running **onstat -g mgm** several times during the day, the administrator sees that, on average, two queries are usually waiting (as in the preceding example). In addition, all queries are running with PDQPRIORITY of 100, which means that only one decision support query will run at the same time. The administrator lowers the PDQPRIORITY configuration parameter from 100 to 33, which allows three queries to run at once.

Chapter 11

The Extended Multiprocessor Release

The Extended Multiprocessor (XPS) database server is designed to run on loosely coupled or massively parallel systems. It extends the basic architecture of the SMP version of INFORMIX-OnLine Dynamic Server to run on very large systems.

This chapter is designed for administrators currently using INFORMIX-OnLine Dynamic Server and exploring the possibility of moving to the XPS database server. It explains the architecture of the XPS database server, describes some important new features, and discusses some performance issues at a high level.

The topics covered in this chapter include:

- What kind of systems can run XPS?
- How the XPS architecture differs from the INFORMIX-OnLine Dynamic Server
- Database features that affect performance
- Data fragmentation issues
- Other performance issues

11.1 XPS HARDWARE ENVIRONMENTS

Symmetrical multiprocessing systems consist of many disks and multiple processors all sharing the same set of memory. At some point in the performance spectrum, adding processors to an SMP system does not improve performance because of limitations in the system bus or with memory. It is at this point, where SMP scalability is not improving, that massively parallel and loosely coupled systems can improve performance.

Even though an SMP system shares memory between processors and disk, the loosely coupled and massively parallel systems that the XPS database server runs on share nothing. You can think of a "shared nothing" system as a collection of stand-alone hardware systems (or *nodes*), each with its own set of disks, memory, and processors. Each node can communicate with other nodes by a high-speed interconnect, which is the key to good performance in a massively parallel system. A high-speed interconnect is usually many times faster than a traditional ethernet connection, ranging from 40 to 160 Mbytes per second.

Now, imagine putting an OnLine system on each node. The database is spread across these nodes as well. What is needed to extend an SMP architecture to a massively parallel architecture is the ability to move messages and data back and forth quickly between nodes and to optimize queries to perform quickly in this kind of environment. These are the main goals of the XPS database server. Since the message handling and query optimization is accomplished internally, understanding how the database server operates in this environment is simply an extension of what you already know about INFORMIX-OnLine Dynamic Server.

The primary advantage of the XPS database server is to spread the work for an individual decision support query across tens or hundreds of nodes. Because of the overhead of passing messages and data across nodes, the XPS server advantages are best seen with queries accessing a very large amount of data.

11.2 THE XPS ARCHITECTURE

Each node has its own OnLine system, known as a *coserver* (see Fig. 11.1). Each coserver has its own root dbspace, logs, shared memory, and virtual processors. Each coserver manages its own chunks and dbspaces. However, to the application developer or user, all the coservers represent a single-system image. The user connects to one coserver (sometimes called a *connection coserver*) to execute an SQL statement. The XPS system handles routing of messages and data between coservers through the High Speed Interconnect.

Coservers can be logically grouped into *cogroups* to allow ease of administration. A common method of creating cogroups is to group all coservers with the same properties (e.g., wide nodes versus thin nodes, single-processor coservers versus multiprocessor coservers) in the same cogroup.

How a Query Is Executed

As in the INFORMIX-OnLine Dynamic Server, a query is parsed and broken into a tree of SQL operators, each performing a specific task. An internal component of XPS, called the request manager, determines how a query will be executed across coservers.

Figure 11.1-A sample XPS system

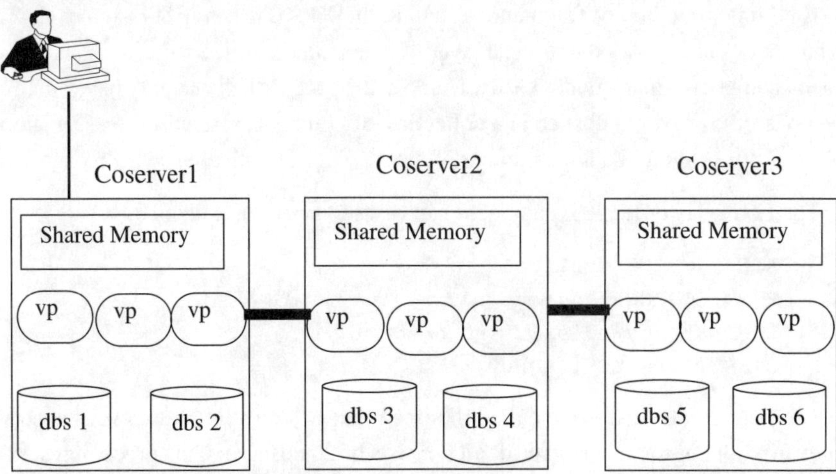

Threads are started for each task and assigned to a particular coserver (see Fig. 11.2). Data are placed into exchanges, a method to pass data between threads and between coservers.

One **scan** thread will start for each fragment to be scanned. In the example in Fig. 11.2, each coserver involved in the query has two fragments that must be scanned. The XPS server decides on the most efficient coserver to start the **sort** and **join** threads.

The **sqlexec** thread starts on the coserver where the application connects.

Figure 11.2-How a query is executed

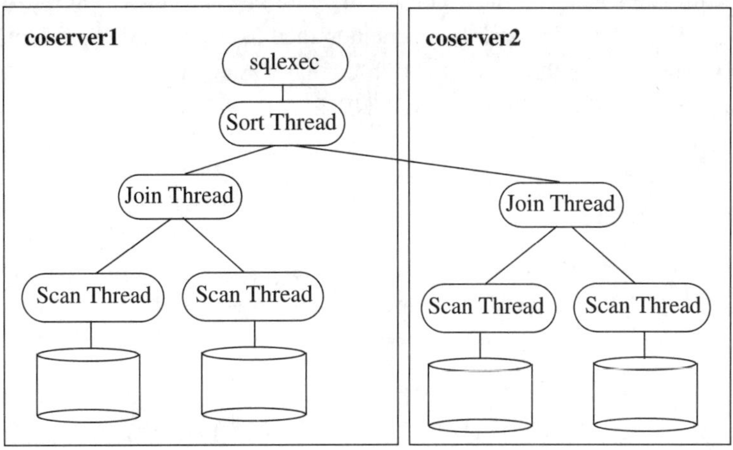

Dbslices

A common method of fragmenting data in the XPS environment is across disks on a large number of nodes. Another logical layer of data storage, called a *dbslice*, can be used to fragment a table over many nodes easily. Unlike a dbspace, which can only have chunks on a single node or coserver, a dbslice is a collection of chunks across coservers. Dbslices can simplify administration of a large number of disks, which is typical in an XPS environment.

The CREATE DBSLICE statement can be used to create a dbslice:

```
CREATE DBSLICE dbslice1
   FROM COGROUP cogroup_all
   CHUNK "/dev/rdisk12v"
   OFFSET 0 SIZE 1000000;
```

This statement creates a dbslice called **dbslice1** that has one chunk on every coserver in the **cogroup_all** cogroup. If **cogroup_all** consists of 20 coservers, the preceding statement will create 20 dbspaces and 20 chunks, one dbspace and chunk on each coserver.

When a dbslice is created, the OnLine system automatically generates dbspace names using a combination of the dbslice name and a sequence number, referred to as the *ordinal* of the dbspace.

Fragmenting a table across the chunks created for **dbslice1** is now a simple matter:

```
CREATE TABLE table1
   col1          integer,
   col2          char(100))
   FRAGMENT BY HASH(column1) in dbslice1;
```

After this statement executes, table1 will be fragmented across all disks included in **dbslice1** (see Fig. 11.3). The hash fragmentation method uses a hash algorithm to specify which fragment to place the row. Although the hash fragmentation method is useful to spread data across multiple disks, the ROUND ROBIN or EXPRESSION fragmentation method can also be used.

Logging Choices

The XPS server requires that all databases be logged. However, since some tables may be read-only, XPS allows different levels of logging for each table within a database. The type of logging determines what operations are acceptable on a table:

- **RAW.** These tables are not logged. Tables with this logging cannot have indexes or constraints. DML (INSERT, UPDATE, DELETE) statements are allowed. No indexes or constraints are allowed.

Figure 11.3-Fragmenting a table across a coserver

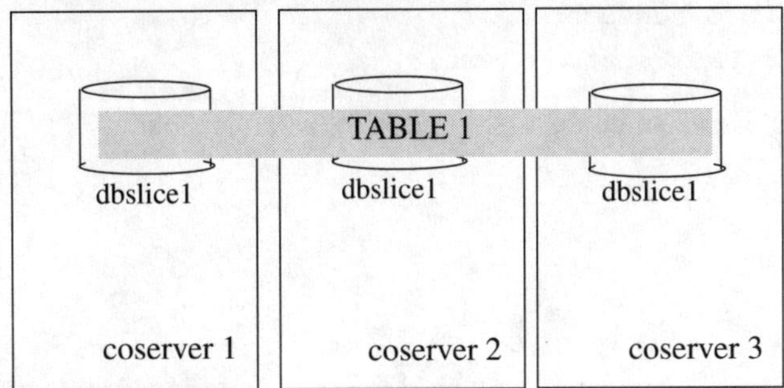

- **STATIC.** These tables are not logged. No DML is allowed (SELECT statements only). Indexes and constraints are allowed.
- **OPERATIONAL.** These tables can be recovered during FAST RECOVERY.
- **STANDARD.** These tables are fully logged, as in previous releases.

These new logging choices allow improved performance for tables that do not need to be logged because of the nature of the data. For example, if a table is completely refreshed nightly, you may want to set logging to RAW or STATIC.

You can specify the type of logging for a table with the ALTER TABLE statement. For example

```
ALTER TABLE t TYPE (RAW)
```

Fast Loads

Most databases on an XPS system will be very large, requiring a fast way to load data. The parallel loading capability of XPS allows you to use an SQL statement to identify tables to be loaded or unloaded. For example, the following statement identifies a new table of type EXTERNAL, which actually refers to three data files that will be loaded in parallel. The three data files are located on coservers 1, 4, and 8, respectively. The load files have the same columns as the CUSTOMER table and are delimited by a pipe character.

```
CREATE EXTERNAL TABLE customer_ext
    SAMEAS customer
    USING(DATAFILES
        (DISK:1:/tmp/load.1,
        DISK:4:/tmp/load.4,
        DISK:8:/tmp/load.8)
    FORMAT "delimited"
    DBDATE "dmy4"
    REJECTDIR "/tmp/reject");
```

To load data from these data files, you can use a simple INSERT statement, such as

```
INSERT INTO customer
SELECT * FROM customer_ext;
```

You can also unload data into the files listed in the external table:

```
INSERT INTO customer_ext
SELECT * from customer;
```

Sampling

In some cases, a query may only need to sample data in a very large table to return an acceptable answer set. The XPS server allows you to choose whether a query will sample data, and how much data will be sampled. Since there are fewer data to read, a query using a sample will finish much more quickly than if it read the entire table.

Obviously, a larger sample will ensure a more accurate answer set. In this example, one million rows are sampled in the ORDERS table:

```
SELECT order_num, count(*)
FROM 1000000 SAMPLES OF orders
GROUP BY 1;
```

In order to perform a query with samples, the administrator must have run UPDATE STATISTICS MEDIUM.

11.3 PERFORMANCE GUIDELINES

As with any sophisticated database server, there are many issues involved in tuning an XPS system. However, because the XPS server is very new, some of the minor configuration parameters and performance guidelines are changing rapidly. This chapter lists the "big picture" performance guidelines for setting up and running a very large database using an XPS system.

Data Fragmentation Issues

The proper data fragmentation strategy can make or break performance in an XPS system. Data must be fragmented in a manner that can take advantage of as many nodes as possible yet prevent as much data shipping between nodes as possible. A join between tables that occurs on one node is sometimes known as a *co-located join*. Co-located joins require that the join tuple be located exclusively on the same coserver. The example in Figure 11.2 shows the use of a co-located join. If a co-located join was not used in this example, the join threads would have had to import data from other coservers to perform the join.

Aim for Co-located Joins   Co-located joins may be difficult to achieve in many queries, and in many cases shipping data from one co-server to another to perform the join may not affect performance adversely because of the efficiency of the high-speed interconnect. However, in some cases where the amount of data being joined is extremely large, co-located joins can improve performance.

To influence the server to perform a co-located join:

- Fragment the tables using the hash fragmentation method on the join keys. For example, for a SELECT statement with a WHERE clause such as **WHERE a.col1 = b. col1**, fragment both table **a** and table **b** by **col1**.
- Fragment the tables with the same number of fragments for each table. An easy way to do this is to use dbslices that were created with the same co-group.

You can determine if co-located joins are occurring for a query by monitoring the received transmissions and send transmissions fields of the **onstat -g xmf** output. A large amount of receive and send transmissions means that there is a large amount of data being transferred between coservers, and co-located joins are probably *not* occurring.

Use Hash Fragmentation   For most tables, the hash fragmentation method is the most useful for large queries. Fragmentation by expression uses more resources than the hash method. The round-robin fragmentation method cannot ensure co-located joins.

The hash column key should not contain a large number of duplicate values. If it does, consider using a composite key that reduces the number of duplicates.

Run UPDATE STATISTICS   As with any INFORMIX database server, it is very important to run UPDATE STATISTICS after data have changed significantly (a large amount of UPDATEs, INSERTs, and DELETEs have occurred). Generally, you will want to run UPDATE STATISTICS MEDIUM for every table.

Configuration Parameters

Most of the new XPS configuration parameters are not performance related. However, many of the INFORMIX-OnLine Dynamic Server parameter guidelines are also applicable to the XPS server.

Set Processor Parameters for the Coserver   When setting the multiprocessor parameters, remember that the parameters apply to the coserver only. If the coserver has only a single processor, set the processor configuration parameters to the following:

```
MULTIPROCESSOR    0
NUMCPUVPS         1
SINGLE_CPU_VP     1
```

For multiprocessor coservers, set the processor configuration parameters to the following:

```
MULTIPROCESSOR    1
NUMCPUVPS         < #number of processors
SINGLE_CPU_VP     0
```

Connecting to Coservers

The **sqlexec** thread runs on the coserver that the application connects to. If all applications connect to the same coserver and run queries simultaneously, you may see a bottleneck in the coserver handling the connections. To reduce this bottleneck you can

- Have applications connect to different coservers.
- Run PDQPRIORITY at 100. This will cause only one query to be processed at one time, which may be more efficient than running multiple queries with a reduced PDQPRIORITY value.

Local Processing

In cases where the SQL statement will read a very large table sequentially (batch processing), you may achieve better performance by breaking up or partitioning the processing yourself. The XPS has an SQL extension that allows you to run a query only on the coserver it is connected to. The local keyword only examines data on the local coserver, bypassing any message passing and other overhead that is required for coordinating coservers.

The following is an example of an SQL statement that retrieves data only from the **customer** fragment on the coserver the application is connected to:

```
select * from local customer;
```

In order to retrieve data from the entire table, you must run a program with this statement on every coserver that contains a customer fragment. Although this method requires more work by a programmer to collect and synthesize the returned data, it can significantly reduce processing time in some cases because

- It eliminates overhead from the database server to collect the data across nodes and ship it to the originating coserver.

- It allows for restartability in case of a node failure. If a node goes down during processing, you need only restart the SQL statement for that node. This advantage can be significant when a failure occurs during a very large query.

11.4 SUMMARY

The XPS database server was designed to improve performance under the following conditions:

- Database sizes are extremely large.
- The majority of queries are decision support (reading and manipulating large amounts of data).

  When planning a move to an XPS server, pay close attention to

- Fragmentation schemes, dbspace and database layout and
- Use of new features

    — Table logging,

    — Local processing, and

    — Sampling.

Index

I

J

K

L

M

T

U

V

Timely & Informative

AVAILABLE ONLY FROM PRENTICE HALL PTR

NEW!
Informix Performance Tuning, Second Edition
Elizabeth Suto

Maximize the performance of your INFORMIX-Online System. This insider's guide to Informix performance has been completely updated to reflect all recent releases of INFORMIX-Online, INFORMIX-Online Dynamic Server and INFORMIX XMP. No matter which release you're running, this book will walk you through all the performance-related issues you need to understand, including: query optimization, database design, disk layout, memory utilization, and processor usage.

1997, 12 pp., cloth, 0-13-239237-2

Informix Stored Procedure Programming
Michael L. Gonzales

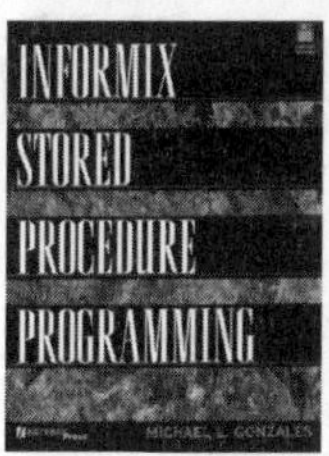

Informix stored procedures, which can be used to dramatically improve the performance of SQL code, tighten security, reduce maintenance of permissions, and maximize data integrity, are often difficult to understand. This book offers numerous examples and illustrations that show how stored procedures can be used to optimize code while improving security and data integrity. Also included is a comprehensive SPL syntax reference, as well as more than 20 stored procedures that can be used or adapted as needed.

1996, 200 pp., Paper, 0-13-206723-4

NEW!
Evolution of the High Performance Database
Informix Software

Industry technologists preview tomorrow's high-performance database solutions. Evolution of the High Performance Database is an up-to-the-minute guide to the most exciting trends in database technology, and how they'll impact you and your organization. In this book, the industry's premier technologists walk you through today's most revolutionary database developments: Databases on the Web, Data Warehousing, and Object Relational DBMSs.

1997, 432 pp., cloth, 0-13-594730-8

INFORMIX-New Era:
A Guide for Application Developers
Art Taylor and Tony Lacy-Thompson

The eagerly awaited Informix-New Era development environment is here, and this book shows exactly how to make the most of its new features. Through practical, hands-on examples, readers will learn how to use the extensive object-oriented capabilities built into NewEra, as well as its improved Window Painter, Menu Painter, and Application Builder Tools. The book also covers how to migrate from Informix-4GL and includes techniques for integrating object-oriented techniques into existing structured code.

1996, 300 pp., Paper, 0-13-209248-4

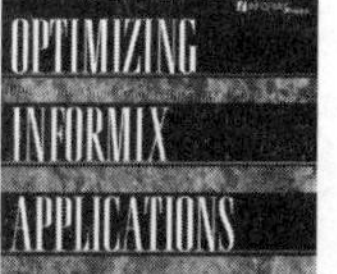

Optimizing Informix Applications

Robert Schneider

Developers and administrators can now improve Informix application and systems performance and increase productivity and system quality with this new title. The book offers detailed tips and shows how to set up an optimization test environment, indexing strategies, and using the Informix optimizer effectively. Also offers a variety of real-world case studies.

1995, 300 pp., Paper, 0-13-149238-1